99

4

The CHILD
WITHIN
CATHERINE MUNROE

The CHILD WITHIN

CATHERINE MUNROE

The Children's Society

MAKING LIVES WORTH LIVING

A VOLUNTARY SOCIETY OF THE CHURCH OF ENGLAND AND THE CHURCH IN WALES

Published by The Children's Society
Edward Rudolf House
Margery Street
London WC1X 0JL

First published 1993

ISBN 0 907324 73 8

Edited by Ann Douglas

The author and The Children's Society are grateful to the Independent Order of Foresters Prevention of Child Abuse Fund UK for their kind contribution towards the costs of producing this book.

CONTENTS

DEDICATION

To my older son who allowed me to practise the skills of being a parent, and to my younger son who allowed me to test those skills to the limit.

Without you my life would be a much less fulfilled, if somewhat quieter, experience.

Luv
Mum
X

ACKNOWLEDGEMENTS

In the completion of the book I would like to thank June for typing my original document, and Ann for editing it so well. Thank you also to Alasdair Gray for the cover illustration.

I would like to thank all my friends and family for their help and support over the past few years, and in particular my social worker and my mother. I would have had great difficulty coping without their support and understanding.

INTRODUCTION

This book is about a ten-year-old boy who came to live with my husband and me after we had been accepted as adoptive parents. It chronicles the first fifteen months of our son's placement with us and the difficulties I encountered in dealing with him during this period. In part I wrote it as a therapy to help me come to terms with what was the most difficult time in my life, a time which challenged not only all my skills as a parent, but also my own sexual identity and my relationship with my husband, my family, my friends.

Paul, in that first fifteen months, permeated, and at times threatened, every aspect of my life. Paul's parents had abused him physically, sexually and emotionally. They had, in effect, taken away his childhood. They also, vicariously, took away part of me. I hope that I will now have the strength to move on from these experiences.

But I have another, more important, reason for putting my experiences on paper. I hope to help other parents and carers and those supporting them in their work with children like my Paul. When Paul was placed with us we received a great deal of support from our social worker. She helped us to understand why Paul was acting in particular ways, she was always ready to listen when I needed to talk things over, and offered practical advice on how to handle Paul. I know I could not have managed without her support and encouragement.

Our social worker would sometimes suggest reading material. However, I found that most of the literature, while being useful in explaining why Paul behaved as he did, had few suggestions about how to cope with his behaviour. Furthermore, the material was written for social workers and did not tell me how other parents and carers dealt with the problems which we were facing. I can assure you it is one thing, and very necessary, to understand why a child is having a tantrum or acting sexually towards you. It is quite another to know what to do about it. This book is my attempt to move beyond the theory to the practice, to suggest practical ways of tackling problems which a disturbed child may present.

I do not pretend to be offering a solution applicable to all children. Paul was a particularly disturbed child with extreme behavioural problems. What worked for him might not necessarily work for other children. Paul is also a particularly perceptive child who is able to verbalise his feelings. The majority of children, I suspect, might feel as Paul does, but may not be able to put their feelings into words; they might, in fact, not even be aware of the reasons behind their behaviour. Thus, while Paul's excesses necessarily forced me to adopt measures more extreme than would normally be the case, his ability to articulate made it relatively easy for me to understand the reasons for his behaviour and to discuss the issues with him.

However, I hope that this book, by looking at one mother's way of tackling her son's problems, will at least help other parents work out possible ways of tackling the problems which their own child presents. I also hope that Paul's verbal skills may give them some insight into the feelings and behaviour of disturbed children. I know I would have found this helpful in my struggle to parent Paul. It is for these reasons that I wish to share my story.

1
PAUL

Our son, Paul, came to us on 19 March 1988 when he was just ten years old. He is an active demanding child with a tremendous capacity to give and receive love. He has a lively sense of humour and has added a great deal of happiness and laughter to our lives. He soaks in new experiences and is happy to 'have a go' at any new activity on offer to him. He is also very brave and has shown tremendous courage in starting again with a new family after family life had let him down and failed him.

From the beginning of Paul's life there were difficulties. His mother had a serious drink problem and his father, although not an alcoholic, often drank too much and had little to do with his son. His parents made no preparations for his birth and it was left to other family members to supply his equipment, clothing and food and do what they could to help. Not much is known of this period in Paul's life but it does seem clear that he was given little attention. He was sometimes left in his pram outside pubs while his mother was inside drinking.

Paul remembers being assaulted as a toddler by his mother, locked in cupboards, neglected and deprived. He sometimes had to steal money from her to buy food. He became adept at manipulating his mother and used tantrums as a way of forcing her to buy him things. He has also told me that he was sexually abused by his mother over a five-year period, from the age of two. These incidents seem to have taken place regularly and involved his mother masturbating Paul and encouraging Paul to touch and masturbate her. At times this was a painful experience for Paul; on other occasions he not only enjoyed it but also initiated sexual advances himself towards his mother. Throughout this period she continued to drink to excess and to be incapable of providing any security or stability for her son.

Paul's father seems to have had a peripheral role in the family. He worked away from home a great deal and it was during these periods that the mother's behaviour was at its worst. However, he was not entirely ignorant of the home situation during his absence. He knew his wife drank and eventually became aware that she hit Paul and locked him in cupboards. Although he does not seem to have actively participated in the sexual abuse, he did watch his wife abusing Paul and sometimes held him down to enable her to do this. He also encouraged Paul to watch him and his wife having sexual intercourse. He was a weak and ineffectual man who constantly deferred to his wife and was therefore unable to offer any protection to his son. Paul's father also had a heart condition, which made him incontinent. He was allowed to urinate all over the house and Paul mimicked him by doing the same. It seems that his mother tolerated this. Paul often slept with his father, despite the fact that he was enuretic.

Paul responded to such gross deprivation and abuse by developing into an extremely manipulative and aggressive little boy. At the age of four he was felt to be out of his parents' control and was asked to leave nursery because of his aggressive behaviour towards other children. It was observed that he had a very strange relationship with his mother, sometimes afraid of her, sometimes manipulating and controlling her.

This situation had worsened by the time Paul started school. From the beginning he had difficulty relating to his peers and he was ostracised by his violent behaviour towards them and by his dirty appearance. Paul was involved in several bizarre incidents of a sexual nature and on occasions was found urinating on passing cars. During his first year at school he was discovered smoking, drinking and stealing. He would often play truant from school and telephone his mother to let her know what he was doing. Once he was found lying on a rubbish tip with a baby's bottle near by. The school were very concerned about Paul and when he was six years old they made a referral to the psychological services and the social services department. Neither organisation seemed to be able to help the family, partly because Paul's mother rarely kept appointments and would not accept any help with her drink problem.

In October 1984 when Paul was six and a half, his father was admitted to hospital with a brain haemorrhage which left him disabled for life. Paul reacted by becoming completely out of control. He broke windows, tore bedding, threw his father's clothes downstairs and refused to wash. In January he was received into care with foster parents for about a week. He then returned home for four months. Paul remembers this period as a continuation and, if anything, a worsening of the abusive situation he had previously experienced. Early in April his father was discharged from hospital, but was confined to a wheelchair. He had become very childish, relating to Paul as a peer and therefore even less able to offer him any protection. Paul also clearly remembers his mother blaming him for his dad's illness. She deeply resented the work involved in caring for her husband and again blamed this on Paul. Paul's behaviour showed a steady deterioration.

On 29 April Paul was received into care again, with the same foster parents, and he began to improve. Access to his parents was arranged but they rarely kept appointments. After six months arrangements were made for him to visit his parents in the family home. These visits were not successful. Paul was obviously afraid of his mother and would try to ensure that his father was between them. His behaviour at school and in the foster home worsened, especially during the day of a visit. Eventually the decision was made—with Paul's agreement—that access should be terminated.

Paul remained in foster care for over a year, during which time application was made to court to have him freed for adoption. Paul's behaviour in the foster home continued to cause problems and, despite attempts to work through these, the foster parents eventually requested that he be moved on. As there were no foster homes available to cope with Paul's particular needs, a place was secured for him at a children's home where he moved in May 1986 when he was eight and a quarter. He remained there until he came to live with us.

Not long after Paul went to the children's home his father had another haemorrhage and died suddenly. When Paul was told, he shed a few tears. He went to the funeral and saw his mother there. But in the weeks which followed he rarely mentioned the subject, and would deliberately block any discussion of his life with his parents. He would talk more frequently about his foster parents.

Initially, Paul settled in well at the children's home, bringing with him lots of toys which he shared. After about a week, though, he began to lash out at the other children in frustration if he could not get what he wanted. He would not join in their play and had a fear of water and dark cupboards. Concern was expressed about the sexual overtures in his behaviour and speech. His manner was like that

of an adult and he enjoyed bossing the staff. He was very affectionate and loved a cuddle, but did not like to share staff with other children. He began to have aggressive outbursts when he would have
to be restrained.

Two people who worked with Paul in the children's home were
Julie, a member of staff, and Jane, a child psychologist. He became
close to Julie and began to share with her some of his feelings about
his past, but at the same time directed the worst of his aggression
and anger at her. His contact with Jane had begun when he had
been referred to Child Guidance and was maintained while he was
in foster care. Paul used his weekly sessions with her to work
through some of his aggressive feelings. He expressed a great deal
of anger that his parents had robbed him of his childhood.

It is clear that Paul had been abused in every conceivable way,
both physically and sexually, and starved of consistent affection and
attention. He lacked any stability or security in his life. In addition,
he had to cope with a sense of rejection by his foster parents, the
death of his father and the problems of institutional care. As a
result, Paul developed into a disturbed and difficult child, who had
little control over his feelings or behaviour, who needed a great deal
of attention but who could not cope with any attention given to others, and who often had tantrums when he would swear and attack
the adults caring for him. He was aggressive towards other children, could be destructive and often responded in a sexual manner.

On the positive side, Paul was a lively and active child who was
capable of giving as well as receiving love. Despite his behaviourial
difficulties he had the gift of making people like him. Surprisingly
he received most empathy from those towards whom his behaviour
was most difficult. This was the quality I first became aware of
when I got to know Paul and it is what makes him such a special
child to me.

What distinguished Paul from many other children who have had
similar backgrounds was that he did not seem to have withdrawn
from life. His anger demonstrated that he was still prepared to feel
the pain of his previous experiences. He had not retreated into hope-
lessness and despair. He had the capacity to put his feelings into
words and make other people sense what his life had been like. This
is why I described Paul as 'brave' at the beginning of the chapter.

2
CATHERINE AND NEIL

Like most adoptive parents, my husband and I had thought long and hard about adopting a child and the effect this would have on our lives. Unlike the stereotyped adoptive parents we were not a childless couple desperate to have a baby. Neil and I had met when we were in our early thirties and we had both been previously married. I had a grown-up son, John, who was at university and living away from home. Neil had no children. We both had demanding full-time jobs which we enjoyed. Neil was a residential social worker in a secure unit and I was a senior social worker. We were an active, fairly independent couple. We liked to 'do our own thing' and had separate friends and interests, although we shared common activities such as hill-walking, bird-watching, skiing. Our home was important but more as a base than in its own right. We were not very organised and did not live to a strictly worked out routine. For example, we ate when we were hungry and when we had time rather than at set hours.

When we began to consider the pros and cons of adopting a child we were both clear, first, that we did not feel the need to have a baby of our own and, second, that we had no desire to adopt a very young infant. At our stage in life, we could not meet a baby's needs without making inordinate sacrifices and changes. At the very least Neil or I would have to give up working for a period and this was something we did not wish to do.

When we looked deeper into our feelings we came to the conclusion that we wanted to adopt an older child and would have most to offer someone of primary-school age. We recognised that such a child was likely to have serious emotional problems but felt that we had the capacity and commitment to help a child work through these problems in the context of family life. We knew that our reasons were not altruistic and that we wanted to commit ourselves to a child who would be capable of giving us some emotional return, though we realised this could be a protracted process.

I feel that any family has to be equally ruthless in assessing their own situation and needs before they apply to adopt or foster a child. We were not naïve enough to believe that an emotionally damaged older child would be able to fit into our home without us having to make changes in our lifestyle. We looked very hard at the changes we would have to make and were willing to make. It would not work, for example, if we had to give up our jobs because this could lead to resentment of the child and probably to a lessening of our commitment. Equally, there is no point in applying to adopt an older child as a second-best option when what you really want is a baby or toddler, because this again could lead to disappointment on both sides. Some children who have been placed in care may be so emotionally damaged that they find it difficult to show any affection or make any deep commitment to a family. Such children often do need a secure family background and there are families who are able to provide this. But these, I feel, will be couples who have either had their own needs to be loved met by having children of their own or do not have such needs and are applying to foster or adopt for more altruistic reasons.

Couples must also work out the possible effect of an adopted child on other children and members of the family and on any close friendships. What type of behaviour would you find intolerable? I believe that such hard thinking is vital if taking a child into your family is going to succeed. It is important to do this before making your application, because once you have applied you are caught up in the assessment process and your desire to pass as prospective parents can often cloud your judgement of what you can give to a child.

Our application to adopt a child was made through a voluntary agency which has a special project to find new families for older children with emotional problems and younger children with mental and/or physical disabilities. Our first interview was with the project leader who told us about the types of children who were waiting for families, the process of an application and the type of support we could expect from the agency. She asked us to discuss in private whether we still wished to apply to adopt through the agency. If we wanted to proceed, we would be asked to attend a preparation group. We did as she suggested and a week later contacted the project to ask for our names to be put forward.

Each preparation group consisted of two workers from the

agency, about six couples who had applied to adopt a child, and two experienced foster parents who came along to share their experiences. The group met once a week for six weeks and focused on issues surrounding child care: the universal needs which children have for love and security and the ways in which emotionally damaged children may have been affected by the lack of these basic needs; the type of background from which these children come and how this might colour their perception of family life; the needs of children with mental and/or physical disabilities and the pressures which these bring to bear in the families who care for them. We saw short videos of some of the children waiting for family placement and were reminded of the likely process of our application and the support offered by the agency. We were then asked to consider again whether we wanted to proceed.

I found the preparation groups very helpful in focusing some of my own feelings about child care and giving me a clearer picture of the type of child and the type of behaviour problems with which we would have to contend. However, discussions tended to concentrate on the theoretical perspective of child care and were aimed at providing information rather than helping us imagine what it would be like to have a child living with us. The presence of experienced foster parents offset this slightly because they were able to describe their specific experiences with children whom they had fostered; but no real attempt was made to get us to examine how we would have felt and reacted in similar situations.

Having said this, I am not certain that prospective adopters would have been open enough to share their thoughts with the agency staff. Although workers were at pains to point out that the group was *not* part of the assessment process but was only a tool to help adopters to decide if they wanted to proceed, I do not think we fully believed this. In any gathering, people form an opinion about each other (I know I did and was aware of a similar process towards myself) and inevitably therefore the agency workers formed opinions of the people in the group. It is hard to believe that, with the best will in the world, their impressions would not enter into the assessment process. The fact that some of the workers in the group would be responsible for assessing us made us feel we had to give the 'right' answers and create the 'right' impression. In this situation people might have felt too threatened to open out and risk exposing their feelings.

It would be a mistake to place expectations on what these groups can never achieve. They served a useful and valid purpose in helping people explore some of the implications of adopting a child; but they left a gap in the preparation. It is important for adopters to know not just what type of behaviour to *expect* but also how they might *feel*, faced with a real live situation. For example, we talked a great deal about aggression, the reasons for it and how we might cope with a child who swore. But we did not explore what we would actually feel if a child punched us and swore at us in the middle of a local shopping centre at peak time or in front of our mother or church minister. The reality is very different from the theory and no amount of understanding can diminish the embarrassment of the situation. These issues can affect the success of otherwise of a placement. I suggest the time for undertaking this deeper work is not at the pre-assessment groups but after the adoptive parents have been approved.

When the preparation groups were finished, the assessment proper began. We were assigned a social worker, Susan, who was responsible for assessing us and would also be responsible for supporting us if a child were placed with us. She explained the sort of questions we would be asked and stressed that the assessment was not a test we would either pass or fail. Rather it was an attempt to help her and us make sure that adoption was right for us and if so the sort of child who would best fit into our family. She stressed that there were no right or wrong answers to the questions she asked, that just as every child is different so too is every adoptive family. People were not excluded simply because their values or beliefs were different. The most important factors she was looking for were an ability to give love and security and a tolerant and flexible attitude towards children.

Neil and I both accepted the validity of what Susan was saying, in the belief that only by working with families could the agency assess whether adoption was right for them. We had met Susan at the preparation groups and were confident that she was not in the business of judging or condemning. However, there is no getting away from the fact that our entering into an assessment was a clear statement that we wanted to adopt a child and that, to a large extent, Susan had the power to say whether or not we had the tolerance and flexibility to be adequate parents of a difficult and damaged child.

The assessment process took about three months and Susan made about ten visits to our home. Most of the interviews involved both Neil and me, but we were also interviewed separately. We talked about our respective backgrounds, our marriage and lifestyle, our motivation in wanting to adopt a child. We also looked at the practical implications arising from our intention to continue working after a child was placed with us. We had to provide two referees whom Susan interviewed. Our police records were checked and we underwent medical examinations. Although we were aware of the purpose of these procedures, we were able to relax and be open with Susan. We were helped because she always gave the impression of being honest in her feelings about our application and that, in general, she accepted us.

The assessment was also a positive experience in its own right. How often does one get the opportunity to spend hours talking about oneself to someone who is paid to be interested and does not ask one to be equally interested in her? It is the egocentric's paradise!

When all the interviews were complete Susan prepared her report for presentation to the Adoption Panel. She shared its content with us and indicated she would support our application. Although the report was a fair reflection of our interviews and we were confident that Susan would represent us fairly, both Neil and I felt that we would like to attend the Adoption Panel ourselves. This was agreed, as a first for the agency who had never before had prospective parents appearing at the Panel.

We had a particular reason for wanting to be present at the Adoption Panel. Before approaching the agency we had applied to adopt a child through a regional council. A similar assessment had taken place but the Adoption Panel decided not to approve us. Naturally this upset us very much, but the decision was made more painful for a number of reasons. First, we were turned down on the basis of facts which we had been assured would not be detrimental to our application. One was that both Neil and I intended to continue working and another was that, although we had been living together for six years, we had only recently married. Further, we did not feel that our social worker had any real empathy with us. He seemed to think it strange that we did not want a baby of our own and chose to adopt an older child. He did not share the assessment report with us so we had no confidence in how he would represent us at the Adoption Panel. Worst of all, it was not policy to be told the date of the Adoption Panel and we did not hear the result until ten weeks after our last contact with our social worker and fully two months after the Panel met. This was despite the fact that Neil and I both tried to find out from the local authority what was happening to our application. We were upset and angry at such secrecy and evasiveness and wanted to know what the social worker had said. The experience made us insistent that we attend the agency's Panel.

On the morning of the Panel I was not so sure we had made the correct decision. Both Neil and I were very nervous. We were worried that we would dry up or say the wrong things, that the Panel would not like us, that a thousand other things could go wrong. It was like an important job interview, taking your driving test, and sitting an examination all rolled into one. I changed several times, not sure what to wear. I did not want to appear too smart in case the Panel thought that I was too fussy to cope with a child who would inevitably be messy and disruptive, but if I dressed too casually the Panel might think I was not serious about the prospect of adoption. I wanted to look like a 'mum' without any real idea of what the Panel saw a 'mum' to be. It was in this state that we drove to Edinburgh to attend the Panel.

We need not have worried. The Chair did her best to put us at our ease and the Panel members were very understanding. I had thought they would ask us 'trick' questions but their questions were in fact simply elaborations of some of the points in the assessment. Both Neil and I had the impression that the Panel was genuinely trying to gain an impression of us as people. We were in the room about twenty minutes and then left to allow the members to consider their decision. Shortly afterwards the Chair informed us that we had been accepted as potential adoptive parents and that Susan would now begin to look for a child for us. What a wonderful feeling! We were both elated and kept saying thank you. The Chair tried to tell us why the Panel had decided to approve us and I can vaguely remember her saying some rather complimentary things about us. But nothing was important after the statement, 'we are pleased to approve you as adoptive parents'. We could not, at that point, think beyond to the implications this approval would have on our lives.

3
THE MATCH

Susan had made it clear to us the type of child she felt would best fit into our home. She was adamant that an emotionally frozen child would not be suitable, that we could not cope with serious behaviourial difficulties if the child was incapable of giving as well as receiving love. About five weeks after our approval Susan told us she thought that she had found such a child and asked if she could come and discuss him with us. In this way Paul was introduced into our lives.

Susan told us that the voluntary agency's central computer, which has details of all approved families and all children awaiting placement registered through BAAF (British Agencies for Adoption and Fostering), had linked us with Paul. Thereafter our papers had been forwarded to Paul's social worker and Paul's papers to our social worker. Both workers felt that it could be an appropriate match. Susan was at pains to assure us that we had the final say on whether we could cope with Paul and that saying no would not be held against us in respect of a future placement.

Susan knew, by this time, something of Neil's and my personalities and that I was more likely to base any judgement on Paul on emotional feelings rather than on an objective assessment of our capacity to cope with his behaviour. So she refused to bring a photograph of Paul to our first discussion, feeling that to do so would give me even less opportunity to be objective. She focused on Paul's background, the problems in his behaviour at the children's home, and in particular his difficult relationship with those women from whom he derives his emotional support. She talked about the aggressive behaviour Julie had to cope with from Paul and the fact that, at times, he behaved in a sexual manner towards her. She provided a picture of a child who would need a great deal of emotional commitment from his female carer, a child who could be loving one minute, violent and aggressive the next, and then make sexual approaches. His relationship towards men tended to be less complicated in that he kept them at arm's length, never sharing any of his loving or his negative side. Susan felt that the man's role would be equally difficult. For much of the time Neil would need to stand on the sidelines, supporting me and perhaps feeling rejected by Paul. We would need to have a strong relationship to cope with Paul's attempts to manipulate and control us. During the interview Susan tried very hard to present the negative and difficult aspects of our role as Paul's parents.

At the time I felt quite frustrated by this approach. I wanted to tell her that she was not presenting us with a picture of a child but merely a catalogue of problems; that she should balance the negative with the positive aspects of caring for Paul. I just could not believe that any child was as bad as Paul seemed to be. On reflection, however, I feel that Susan was right. I tend to be enthusiastic and optimistic. This helps me to cope with situations but tends to make me dismiss difficulties. If Susan had given us a more 'rounded' picture of Paul I would have exaggerated the positives and minimised the negatives. Again, although I was desperate to see a photograph of the child we were talking about, I think Susan was right to refuse. Paul is a very attractive child, with dark hair and an endearing smile. One photograph of him and no amount of problems would have mattered. I would have felt like rushing to the children's home and bringing him back.

After the interview Susan left us some reports to read and asked us to consider carefully whether we felt that we could cope with Paul. The next step, if we wished to go ahead, would be to arrange an interview with Julie and with Paul's social worker, David. Again she emphasised that there was no obligation on our part to feel that we had to proceed.

Hardly was she out of the door than I was enthusing that Paul sounded just right for us. Neil, I am thankful to say, can be more cautious and he insisted on us reading carefully through the reports and considering their implications. We did this over the next few days, with me trying to curb my initial enthusiasm and be more objective. I am not sure that I entirely succeeded, but Neil and I certainly gave a lot of thought to how we might deal with the various behaviour problems Paul might display. We felt we could cope with bad behaviour directed specifically at ourselves, but there were three other areas which could cause us problems. First school: we recognised that many disturbed children have difficulties at school and that if we had to take time off work to deal with these, this could create pressure on our jobs, particularly if Paul was sent home from school. Secondly, we had decided to use my mother as a child minder for the hours between school and our return from work. My mother has fairly fixed ideas of how children should behave and would not be able to cope well with swearing and aggression. Thirdly, we have a dog and cat of whom we are very fond. The dog is particularly defenceless and we knew that we would be very angry with anyone who hurt him. We decided that we would raise these three issues in our next discussion about Paul.

At the next interview I got what I wanted - a photograph of Paul and a more 'rounded' picture of him. This interview, which comprised Susan, David, Julie, Neil, myself and my son John, had a different emphasis to previous ones. We were aware that Julie had a special relationship with Paul and that, if Julie liked us, there was a good chance that Paul too would like us. We were anxious to be as natural as possible to give her a true picture of what we were like. I think by this time we were less concerned to prove that we were adequate parents and more concerned about Paul and the damage which could be done to him if we misled people to believe that we were right for him when we were not.

We liked Julie from the moment we met her and she too seemed to like us. She was very open and honest with us, providing some of the 'meat' to the reports we had received from Susan. She described a child who was extremely demanding and who had difficulty sharing adults with other children. He had aggressive temper tantrums which meant that he had to be restrained at times to avoid hurting himself and others. These she felt were primarily attention-seeking devices because they forced staff to intervene to control Paul. On a personal level he particularly disliked Julie paying attention to other children and would often kick or hurt her. At one stage Paul had indicated that he had a 'secret' he would like to share with her, but only if she promised not to tell anyone else. Julie told us that she had made this promise, although she knew that she could not keep it. Paul never did tell Julie his 'secret' but he did hint that it was of a sexual nature. He probably knew she could not keep her promise and therefore did not trust her enough to share his experiences with her.

After this episode Paul's aggression towards Julie increased and his 'friendly' approaches became more sexual. When she tried to explain to Paul that she liked him but that her relationship to him was that of an adult to a child, he accused her of 'baby snatching'. Julie found both the sexual and the aggressive elements of Paul's behaviour very distressing and at times felt she could not carry on working with him, despite considerable support from fellow workers. Nothing she did to help Paul seemed to have any effect. She often felt that his behaviour was getting worse rather than better.

On the positive side, though, Julie described a lively, interesting child who could be loving and affectionate on his own and polite and well-behaved in public. She said that it was a pleasure to take him out. When she talked about Paul it was clear that, despite his behaviour, he meant a great deal to her. She had even considered applying to adopt him herself, but she had a daughter of the same age and was aware that the two children would have difficulty in coping with each other. I felt encouraged that, despite his difficulties, Paul had enough positive, loving qualities to inspire warmth and affection. I was to get this impression time and again from several other people.

David, Paul's social worker, also seemed very fond of Paul, but it was clear that Paul had never displayed any of the negative side of his personality to David nor shared any of his deeper feelings with him. David recognised and accepted that his relationship with Paul was fairly superficial. The difference between Paul's relationship with David and with Julie highlighted the likely relationships which Paul was to have with Neil and myself, something for which Susan had prepared us.

We also heard about some of the other workers involved with Paul, in particular his psychologist, Jane. We were told that, through play, he had indicated to Jane that his mother had physically and sexually abused him, although he had never verbalised this. It was suggested that we should meet Jane and also attend some of the regular co-ordination meetings at the children's home.

Meanwhile Julie and David had reassured us about the potential areas of stress which Neil and I had identified. They felt that Paul's major problems would be with me and not my mother, that there was no history of Paul being aggressive to animals, and that his behaviour and performance in school were reasonable.

Our meeting with David and Julie was probably the most significant which we attended in relation to Paul. I think this was partly because we met in our house, the setting where we felt most relaxed and at ease; also the meeting was informal, involving only a few people. But, most important, Julie was able to describe in considerable detail specific incidents which highlighted Paul's behaviour. This helped us to focus on how he actually behaved and to visualise how we might cope with him in similar situations.

The behaviourial difficulties we knew we would have to face in no way put us off adopting Paul. If anything, they increased our desire to go ahead. After the meeting Neil and I discussed all we had been told. Paul's photograph was placed carefully in a central place on our mantelpiece. We were beginning to make an emotional commitment to him and to visualise him being part of our home.

This is probably a bit like the process which natural parents undergo. As their emotional commitment to their baby develops with pregnancy, so did ours to a child with the progress of the adoption assessment, especially once we had been 'introduced' to Paul. Also, like natural parents, we were slightly romantic. We *knew* that Paul would be difficult, but not how his behaviour would make us *feel*. They *know* their baby will cry during the night, but not how tired they will *feel* when they have been up every night for months. No amount of preparation can fully prepare you for the reality but meetings like the one we had with Julie and David certainly helped. Perhaps this is the best that can be achieved.

The next few weeks were the most frustrating for us. We were desperate to meet this child we had heard so much about, but local authority policy prevented us from doing so. We first had to attend a co-ordination meeting. Then an Adoption Panel had to discuss whether we and Paul were matched, and the director of social work had to approve. The co-ordination meeting was held in the children's home. It was another large group and we felt nervous and on trial. However, we met Paul's psychologist, Jane, and were immediately struck by her warmth and understanding. She told us that Paul was a very damaged child but also a very special child, who would challenge anyone caring for him, but who would also amply reward any effort made to help him come to terms with his past. She asked us if meeting all these people was like meeting one's mother-in-law for the first time. It wasn't. It was like meeting ten mothers-in-law! However, everyone was very kind and tried to put us at ease.

After the meeting we were shown round the children's home and taken to see Paul's room. At first I was keen to do this so as to find out as much as possible about Paul, but then I began to feel uncomfortable. I felt as if I were prying into his life without being given permission.

Two things helped us to cope with the waiting. The first was that Neil and I were invited to a Christmas party which Paul was due to attend. We were told that we could meet Paul, but could give him no indication of who we were. This was not an arbitrary decision but was to protect Paul from possible disappointment. Children were not told about their possible families until all the meetings had taken place and approval had been granted, in case anything should go wrong and they had their hopes raised to no avail. We leapt at the chance to see Paul. Unfortunately Neil had to go into hospital, so I went to the party by myself.

I would like to say that my first sight of Paul was a momentous occasion and that we immediately felt an affinity. However, this was not the case. I wanted to say something significant to him, but I didn't. He arrived with his social worker, an ordinary boy who was more interested in what there was to do than in the myriad of adults present. I thought he looked much nicer than his photograph and I bored my social worker by going on and on about how lovely he was. But there was no great rush of feeling "this is going to be my son". He came across as a fairly typical boy who was interested in watching videos, playing games, eating as much as possible and hoping to get something nice from Santa. He did not really stand out from the fifty other boys at the party. To my credit I managed to stay in the background and the only remark I made to him was at the end when I asked him what he had got from Santa. Naturally Paul cannot remember even seeing me at the party although he was, much later, amused when I told him how I met him there, how I bored Susan and how I tried to follow him round without being noticed.

After the party I went immediately to the hospital and told Neil in detail everything that had happened, what Paul looked like, what he had done, how he had responded. I said he was lovely, had a gorgeous smile, and was nothing like the disturbed, aggressive boy who had been described to us. In fact, if anything, he was quiet and polite.

Secondly, we were asked to prepare an album to give Paul some idea of what we were like. It would be handed to him before he met us and would help to make the first meeting less traumatic. We had

18

a lot of fun compiling the book. We searched through our old snap-shots for pictures of things we liked doing and we took photographs of John, the cat and dog, our town, the house, the school Paul would attend, the local park, in fact everything we thought Paul would be interested in seeing. Then we wrote a story round the best to illustrate our family's lifestyle. Neil and I had endless arguments over which photographs to use and how to word our story. It became important that we got it right.

Eventually our match with Paul was approved and at last we would meet him. It had taken approximately six months since applying to the agency to reach this point (eighteen months since our initial application to the regional council). We felt as though we were at the end of a hurdle race and had managed to win first prize. But there was still one more hurdle to jump over — another meeting. This was a planning meeting to map the out introductory phase of Paul's placement with us. It involved all those who were at the previous meetings and was held in the children's home. Surprisingly, I felt more relaxed than at previous meetings and much more confident about putting forward my own point of view. This was partly because now that we had been approved we felt much less on trial. The meeting was primarily a procedural device to plan our introductions to Paul in the most appropriate manner. But also it was very important to me that these introductions went well and I felt that I too had a right to say what I thought should happen. If occasionally I felt emotional it was from relief at having reached this point and because of the enormity of the step we were planning.

The meeting decided that the introductions to Paul should be spread over a period of a month, with us having increasing contact with him. The first was to take place in the children's home and Paul would be told about us and given our album the previous day. This would ensure that he had enough time to ask questions about us but not enough to become too agitated about meeting us. Thereafter we would visit the children's home weekly midweek and also see Paul at weekends. The first weekend we would take Paul out, the following weekend he would visit our home, the next he would spend a night with us, and the last weekend before moving he would stay with us. Another meeting was planned for the last week of the introductions to assess whether these were going well and whether the date planned for Paul to move was still appropriate.

The night before Neil and I were due to meet Paul we telephoned the children's home to see how he had responded to the news and were told that he had seemed pleased that a family had been found for him and was quite taken with our book. He had shown it to all the children and staff and had put it in his schoolbag to take to his teacher. All in all this was a much more positive response than we had been led to expect. Paul's psychologist and social worker had felt he might initially be very worried about meeting a family and the prospect of leaving the children's home.

18 February was D-day. Work seemed to drag until it was time to go and meet Paul. Both Neil and I were very nervous about how to approach this meeting. What would Paul make of us? I was in a quandary, just as I had been at the Adoption Panel, about what to wear to make myself look like a 'mum' and whether to put on make-up. It would be hard enough for us to know what to say to Paul and I was anxious that our appearance should do nothing to create barriers.

4
INTRODUCTIONS

I shall never forget the first meeting with Paul. It did not begin very well. We were caught in a traffic jam on the way to the children's home and were late. This made us even more agitated than we would otherwise have been and, as I rushed up the path carrying a bag of sweets in one hand and dragging the dog with the other, I felt sure that Paul would be annoyed with us and that this would sour our first meeting. I only hoped that we could use the dog to break the ice and that the sweets would help as they did with most children.

I need not have worried. As Neil and I walked into the room, we saw Paul sitting in a chair with our book at his side. His social worker, David, and his key-worker in the children's home, Willie, were sitting talking at the other end of the room. I approached Paul, said 'hello' and handed him the sweets. Neil also said 'hello' and we sat down beside him. Paul immediately put the sweets to one side and started talking to us. He expressed a passing interest in the dog but was much keener to talk to Neil and me and to tell us about himself. We became so engrossed that we almost forgot about the other people in the room and about the time. Over an hour passed before Willie offered us a coffee and we realised how long we had been there. Throughout Paul had been taking an active part in the conversation and I was amazed at how easy he was to talk to and how interesting. Even at this meeting his sense of humour showed in some of the 'off the cuff' remarks he made and his liveliness was obvious from the fact that, although he spent all the time sitting and being attentive to us, he was never still for a moment. He was remarkably honest and open with us, even sure enough of himself to make a few cheeky remarks about the colour of my hair and Neil's moustache and beard.

After Willie had broken the intimacy of this first meeting, we spent the next hour talking not only to Paul but also to him and David. Paul played for a while with our dog, Bonzo. He showed us around the home, giving us a guided tour of his room and introducing us to some of the other children.

Both Neil and I were elated at the success of this first visit and on the way home could talk of nothing else. I was amazed at how confidently Paul conducted himself and how he seemed to respond so positively to us. I was also pleased that he had not been very interested in the sweets or in the dog but seemed to realise that these were not important if he did not get on well with Neil and me. This demonstrated an insight which I would not naturally have expected of a ten-year-old child. In short, Paul had captured my imagination, my respect and my interest. I was enchanted by him and could fully appreciate why his psychologist had described him as a 'special child'. I do not think Neil felt the same. He was pleased that our first visit had been a success but saw Paul more as an ordinary boy whom he quite liked but for whom he experienced no real sense of attachment. Despite the difference in our feelings we could not wait until Saturday when we would be able to spend the entire day with Paul. We had chosen to go to Stirling because this was familiar to Paul and we felt that he would probably be more relaxed in his own environment.

My son, John, took the positive step of making a surprise visit home from his university in England that weekend in order to meet Paul. I had not really expected this because, although John is close to me, he has his own life to lead and I had expected that he would see Paul as largely peripheral to that life. The fact that he came home clearly demonstrated to me that this was not so and that, as a member of the family, he wanted to be involved in our plans to adopt Paul. I was pleased that Paul and John would meet and knew that John would try hard to put Paul at his ease.

I suppose the day itself followed the classic pattern of such introductory visits. We met Paul at the appointed time and drove to Stirling. After lunch at the local burger bar we went to Stirling castle. Paul was quite excited and, although he tried very hard to remain calm and take an interest in the castle and its history, it was clear that what he really wanted to do was to run around and play hide-and-seek in the castle grounds. Within a short time he was behaving like a typical ten year old. We happily indulged Paul and very much enjoyed seeing the castle through his eyes as a "great place to play games". But it did emphasise to us that our days of doing our own things when we went out were over and that from now on we would have to take into consideration the needs of a live-ly boisterous child.

During the day we spent some time in the shops looking for a present to give Paul for his birthday. (We had decided not to join him on the actual day, feeling he would prefer to spend it with the staff and children of the children's home, whom he obviously knew better than us.) I also asked Paul to help me choose a birthday card for my mother whose birthday was in February too. His choice was startling, a suggestive card entirely inappropriate for a daughter to send to her mother. This was the first time Paul demonstrated to us how the sexual abuse he had suffered affected his perception of family relationship.

Before returning to the children's home, we decided to go for a quick bite to eat. We drove to an hotel on the outskirts of Stirling, parked the car and started to get out. Suddenly a voice from the back of the car said, "Where are you going?" When I explained we were going to get something to eat in the hotel, Paul said, "I'm not going in there". I immediately attributed this to a deep fear of alco-hol, that he associated hotels with people drinking and, given his parents' drink problem, was worried that we would be drinking. But Paul went on, "That's a place for snobs and I'm not a snob". Although I told him it was not a posh hotel, he insisted, "I'm not going in. You go if you want. I'll stay in the car." We gave in, asked Paul if he knew any non-posh restaurants and, on his advice, went to a café in his local town for fish and chips. My first reaction to this was to feel pleased that Paul was sufficiently relaxed with us to be able to say what he wanted; my second was how to avoid eating out in burger bars for the next few years and how to change Paul's feel-ings about restaurants.

This incident highlights three important points. First, although I was trying to tune into Paul's feelings about things, I was looking for meanings to his actions which related to what I knew of his background, whereas he saw the situation in quite a different way. I related his dislike of the hotel to his parents' abuse of alcohol, whereas Paul was concerned about his perception of himself as not being a 'snob'. I think I also underestimated what he was saying, feeling that his reason for not wanting to go into the hotel was not as good as my reason, that if his reason had been related to his past it would have been more worthy of sympathy. This is wrong. We have to be aware of how children see themselves and this is at least as important as their past and equally affects their behaviour. Secondly, the episode brought home to us how different Paul's experiences were to ours and how this would show itself in many small as well as large ways. Thirdly, although I tried to understand Paul and was in the short term prepared to alter my actions to accommodate his feelings, my longer term aim was to encourage him to alter his behaviour to suit my feelings and my lifestyle. To a certain extent this is inevitable when a child comes into your home, relates primarily to your family and friends, adjusts to your standards. But it is important to be aware of this anomaly, especially at times when the child is difficult and seems unwilling or unable to change his behaviour. You might see the issue as simply the difference between, say, going into a burger bar or a restaurant. He might see it as an attempt, by you, to change his basic personality and thereby reject the person he is.

On the whole the rest of the introductory visits went well. We also spoke on the telephone. These conversations were surprisingly good with Paul chatting at some length about what he had been doing since we last saw him. The Thursday evening visits to the children's home were the most difficult. Neither Neil nor I felt relaxed and Paul seemed unsure how to fit us into the structure of the establishment. It was as though we were interrupting and imposing ourselves on the life of the home. We tended to spend most of the time in the visitors' sitting room, occasionally taking the dog for a walk or talking to the staff and the other children.

On one of the visits Paul announced that he was taking part in a school show and asked if we wanted to come and see him perform. Naturally we were delighted and on our way to the local town hall where the show was taking place I asked what he was going to do in the show and was puzzled at the vagueness of his reply. As he is generally a very articulate child I assumed he wanted to surprise us. When we arrived at the hall I asked Paul where he would be changing. He became even more evasive and then announced that he was merely a reserve and that as everyone had turned up for his act he need not perform. Gradually it dawned on me that Paul had never been in the show and had lied to us because he wanted to see it and was not certain that we would agree unless he had a good reason for us being there. Neil and I gently told Paul we knew about his 'lie', but understood why he had behaved in this way, that it must be difficult to know how to ask us to go somewhere with him, especially if he thought we might not agree. We explained that, had he told us the truth and invited us to the show, we would have been happy to attend whether or not he was performing. He had a right to express his own wishes and we would be willing to accommodate his activities, just as we hoped he would take an interest in ours. Paul seemed quite relieved at our response and, although verbally he continued to assert that he had told us the truth, his attitude indicated that we were correct in our assessment.

This was to be a continuing feature of Paul's behaviour. He often tells lies to cover up some misdemeanour and when found out will not admit to lying. He will only tell more lies and angrily refuse to accept any fact which contradicts his assertions. In extreme situations he will even manipulate the discussion to try and make me justify myself to him. But if I make it clear to Paul that I know he is lying, he may eventually acknowledge, perhaps by a smile, perhaps by his silence, that I am correct. I have now decided that a direct admission is not necessary and that any acknowledgement is sufficient to enable me to focus on the reason for the lie and not to be diverted into senseless arguments of the "you're telling lies", "no, I'm not" variety.

The evening of the school show highlighted another of the less pleasant sides of Paul's personality. On the way home he asked if he could have some chips. We agreed and so he arrived back at the children's home with fish, chips and some juice. The moment he got into the house he started shovelling the food into his mouth as quickly as possible. Some of the other children asked Paul for a chip but this only made him eat more greedily. I realised then this was an extreme example of what Paul did with most food, gobbling everything up at once and never leaving anything for later. Many children in care probably do this, in the belief that the longer you have something the more likely it will be taken away from you. But whatever the reason it was a disgusting habit and we hoped that as he settled with us and realised that things were his to keep he would not need to act in this way.

The weekend after Stirling, Paul visited our home for the day. We asked him to bring our album with him and we took him to the various places illustrated in it, including his future school. This was seven miles from our home, so as to be near my mother who would be minding Paul after school hours until we returned from work. We had to enrol Paul in a school near her for our childminding arrangements to be viable. We thought that the distance might upset Paul because his present school was only a few minutes' walk from the children's home, but he made no fuss and seemed to accept the reason for our choice. We also introduced him to my mum and from the beginning he got on well with her. This no doubt helped him to accept our arrangements.

On the next visit, his first overnight with us, I took Paul to buy his school uniform. This was the first time I had been out with Paul on my own and I was quite anxious how he would respond. We had explained to him that in his new school most of the children wore uniforms and that we expected him to do likewise. Paul said that he had never worn a uniform before and was not keen on the idea. Only snobs wore uniforms. We stuck to our guns and eventually he agreed. This was the first real confrontation we had had with Paul and I wondered if he would use it to create a scene in the shop. In view of our knowledge of Paul's behaviour, I expected this, but in fact he agreed quite readily to being measured and having clothes chosen for him. What dumbfounded me, however, was his extremely babyish behaviour. He started crawling around the shop on his hands and knees, only standing up to be measured. I did not know what to do. He was not creating a scene, but he was behaving extremely oddly. We had been told that Paul might regress when he came to live with us but I did not expect anything as pronounced. Neither did I expect him to regress in the middle of a shop surrounded by other shoppers and shop assistants who, I was certain, were wondering why a ten-year-old boy was crawling about like a baby and blamed me for not having more control over him. I was in a quandary. Should I tell him to get up, with the risk that he might see this as denying him the right to regress? Or should I let him continue, thereby giving him the impression that such behaviour was acceptable? There was also the possibility that his reaction, if I told him to get up, would make us even more noticeable. In the end I took the coward's way out and did nothing except complete my purchases as hastily as possible and get out of the shop.

This incident unnerved me because it brought home to me some of what we had been told about Paul and made me realise that I could never be sure of his reaction in even the most mundane of situations. It was not just Paul's 'bad' behaviour that would cause problems for us. I was also upset by my own inability to determine what to do for the best. This was partly, I have to admit, because I wanted to preserve appearances and was concerned what other people would think. It is one thing to cope with this sort of behaviour in your own home, quite another in a public place. It is also one thing to hear that a child might regress and understand his need to do this and quite another to have to cope with it actually happening. There was also the question of why Paul was behaving like this. I did not think he was doing it to wind me up but because he simply did not know how to act in a situation which I took for granted.

There were no such traumas on the next visit. We had decided to tackle the eating-out issue. It was Neil's birthday and we told Paul that, in our family, we celebrated birthdays by going out to a place chosen by the person whose birthday it was. We said that Neil wanted to go to a local restaurant and wanted Paul to join the celebration. There was no protest and on the day of the treat Paul arrived at our house with his best clothes, even though we knew he did not like dressing up and "looking like a right little snob".

We had chosen a family restaurant which was not too up-market and Paul's behaviour was excellent. He sat quietly, ate his meal in a reasonable manner and did his best to talk in a calm and intelligent fashion. He also seemed to enjoy himself, being allowed to choose what he wanted from the menu and in particular the waitress calling him 'sir'. It was lovely to see him so happy and amused. He kept saying to us "Call me sir" and "Sir would like some ice cream now". At the end of the evening he informed us in a serious voice that he might get used to the idea of being a snob. Neil and I could hardly refrain from laughing and we remember this meal as a special occasion.

Two other very positive things happened during the introductory period. The first occurred when we arrived one day at the children's home to be met by Paul who thrust an object into my hand. "This is for you. I made it at school. It's for Mother's Day. It's probably rubbish." He looked so tense, as if wondering how I would respond. I looked down at what he had given me. It was a swan carved out from a cake of soap, nestling in a cardboard basket. A lump came to my throat and for a couple of seconds I could hardly speak. Here was a child whose experience of family life could only be described as abysmal, handing me (his prospective mother) a token of hope for a future with us. I thanked Paul and said that I would always treasure his gift to me. I still have that swan and still marvel at Paul's courage in giving it to me when it would have been so much easier to discard it or give it to one of the workers in the children's home.

The second positive sign came during discussions about the name Paul would like to be called and what he should call us. We had told him that, although we wanted to adopt him, we would never insist on him changing his surname to ours or calling us mum and dad. We would be pleased if he did, but the most important thing was that we should all settle down well together, irrespective of names. To avoid putting any pressure on Paul ourselves, we suggested that he might discuss with Willie or Julie which name he wanted to be called at his new school. Towards the end of the introductions, Willie told us that Paul wanted to adopt our name and also that he would like to call us mum and dad, but was shy about doing so for the first time. Both Neil and I were touched by this. Here was another sign that Paul was prepared at least to try to integrate with us. We felt that we ought to help Paul over the initial hurdle and should not perhaps have put the onus on him in initiating the discussion. On the next visit we broached the subject and told Paul how pleased we were to hear that he wanted to use our surname and to call us mum and dad. At our suggestion he tried out our new titles a few times during that day to get used to saying them. Soon he was calling us mum and dad.

Towards the end of the introductory period we had our meeting with Paul's workers. Everyone was pleased at the positive response Paul had made during the introductions and it was unanimously agreed that the timetable for his placement with us should be as planned. The question of support was then discussed. Financial assistance in the form of an Approved Adoption Allowance had already been authorised, as well as help with the cost of furniture and clothing. It was now agreed that we would need regular support both from Paul's social worker and our own and that Paul should continue to see his psychologist. We were assured that we could contact our social worker at any time and were given home telephone numbers of staff at the agency in case help was required outside office hours. Neil and I knew, despite all the positive signs during the introductory period, that there were bound to be problems and we welcomed this plan of support.

The introductions were now over. In general, they had gone well. We felt we were getting to know Paul and, although we were aware that his behaviour would not always be so good, we were keen for him to come and live with us. However, if the introductions were intended to give us an idea of what it would be like when Paul lived with us, they did not succeed. Nor could they. Paul's visits were just that, visits. They did not have the permanence to test what it would be like to have Paul as a member of the family. Over and above this I was unsure of my role as parent and what the rules should be. What sort of behaviour would I have to accept as part of Paul's disturbance, at least in the short term, and what behaviour would be totally unacceptable? I was probably trying too hard to understand Paul and thereby not acting naturally. I was also impatient to get the introductions over and to begin living with Paul.

On a more mundane level the four-week introductory period was extremely tiring. Our lives were almost consumed by Paul. We seemed to be constantly dashing back and forward to the children's home, being with him, telephoning him, analysing our latest meeting and discussing how to handle the next. I had great difficulty in thinking of anything else. It was an exciting time but disorientating. We felt our lives were not really our own. Practical tasks like housework and shopping had to be squeezed in. By the end of the introductions we were glad, not just that Paul was coming to live with us, but that the trips to the children's home were coming to an end and we could return to some degree of normality.

What follows is a description of the first year or so of Paul's life with us. I have divided this time into various sections for convenience: they do not signify major developments. There certainly was a change in Paul's behaviour over the whole period but this was a gradual process, not a series of improved behaviour leaps. If Paul or Neil had been telling the story, they might have divided it in a different way.

5
HOME

On 19 March at 9.55 a.m. we arrived at the children's home to take Paul home. We thought we were well prepared. He had been enrolled at school and his uniform and new clothes had been bought. John's room had been cleared, all its cupboards emptied, ready for him. We had bought new bedding and even a welcoming present, a Garfield teddy which we put in the bed with the idea that it might comfort him on the first few nights in his new home. We were aware that this would be a difficult time for Paul but felt we had done all we could to help him settle.

Neil and I had spent some time talking about how we would approach this first weekend and accepted that we would have to build up a relationship at Paul's own pace. This might be a prolonged process and we were determined not to 'crowd' him. We were also aware that Paul was moving into our home and that, while we would need to alter our lifestyle, the greatest adjustments would be made by Paul, who had never known normal family life. One adjustment, though, we were determined to make in our lives was to establish set times for meals. We knew that Paul would not be used to our lack of routine.

I had an idea in my mind of what the first few days would be like — the classic picture of a child coming into the house, being quiet and withdrawn, then going through the 'honeymoon' phase before beginning to test us out. I did not expect to feel physical or emotional closeness for some time and was prepared to work at helping Paul to develop a commitment to us. I understood that the finality of leaving the children's home might increase Paul's apprehension of coming to live with us.

All these thoughts must have been on my mind as we arrived at the children's home but they were very much submerged by a feeling of excitement. When we arrived one of the children began shouting, "Paul, they're here, they're here". He had obviously been asked to look out for us, but as we went inside Paul strolled up doing his best to look as though he was taking all this excitement in his stride. He helped to load his belongings into the car, before going back to say a very matter-of-fact goodbye to the other children and staff. I had taken some sweets for Paul to give the children as a parting gift and he seemed quite embarrassed, as though we were trying to make more of the parting than he wanted.

We had decided to spend the weekend around the house, to allow Paul to get used to his new home and to settle down before starting school. I helped him to unpack and was sad to see his 'belongings' — a case full of toys, mostly old, and a few clothes. Apart from a good-luck statue which had been given to him when he left the children's home, there was nothing which could be called personal, nothing which he seemed to treasure, either from his foster parents or his natural parents. The unpacking also helped me to unravel a mystery which had puzzled me during the introductions. On every visit Paul wore the same trousers and, except on Neil's birthday when we went out to dinner, he never brought a change of clothes with him. I had wondered if, as children do, he had taken a particular liking for these trousers and refused to wear anything else. Instead I discovered that, apart from his smart pair, they were the only trousers he possessed and that the clothes in his case were new and obviously bought to kit him out for the move to our house. It certainly put paid to any idea I had that children in care were well provided for in a material sense.

When I left Paul to get settled into his room, he spent some time sticking his posters on the walls, a way of imprinting his own identity on the room. He arranged and rearranged them until he was satisfied with the results. Then he 'discovered' Garfield. Instead of being pleased, he did not know what to do or think. He did not immediately realise that Garfield was a gift, nor did he ask who the teddy belonged to. To hide his uncertainty he returned it to the bed and pretended to be unaware of its existence. We explained that Garfield was a welcoming present and ignored the fact that he had deliberately lied about not noticing it. I realised that Paul's lie was a self-protective device. I am sure that he had hoped that Garfield was for him but wanted to protect himself from the disappointment of finding that it belonged to someone else. He was obviously not used to surprises and the episode made me realise that I could not assume that Paul would know things which other children took for granted.

For the remainder of the weekend things went according to plan. We had a fairly quiet time. We spent Saturday in the house and on Sunday Paul helped Neil with the gardening and we took the dog for a walk. Paul seemed quite happy. His behaviour was fairly reasonable, although even from the beginning he was very noisy and could not sit still for a minute. This did not pose any particular problems but it was so different from our usual peaceful existence that it took us some time to adjust to the fact that this 'noise' was here to stay.

Paul did not seem to know how to act in the house and would jump from chair to chair without any thought of the damage he might be doing. He spent literally hours sliding down the stairs, most of this time inside a sleeping bag but also on his back with no protection. By the end of the weekend he had carpet burns, yet when I asked him if sliding downstairs hurt him, he was emphatic that he felt no pain. His obvious enjoyment confirmed this and reminded me of one of the issues raised at the preparation groups that disturbed children are often not aware of their own bodies and do not feel pain, or cold or hunger, in the way non-abused children do. This certainly seemed to be the case with Paul. Neither Neil nor I attempted to stop Paul from sliding downstairs. It could not really be described as 'bad' behaviour and we felt it might be his way of settling into the house, though I did remind Paul, from time to time, that he must be feeling some discomfort and that the remedy was to stop sliding downstairs. I hoped that this would re-enforce the idea that pain was connected with behaviour and that he had the power to make pain go away.

Another amazing feature of Paul's behaviour at the weekend was his need for physical contact with me. His first approach was to ask me to playfight. I agreed to this because I felt that any form of physical contact would help to encourage the growth of our relationship and that playfighting might be the only form Paul could accept at this stage. I also hoped that if I made sure that it was just play and that Paul was not hurt he would begin to trust me. However, it was Paul who sometimes hurt me. He seemed to find it very difficult to know when to stop.

By Saturday evening Paul moved on from this aggressive form of contact to wanting cuddles. Again his behaviour was extreme. He wanted bear hugs and to jump up and put his legs round my waist and his arms round my neck. He followed me about, hardly letting me out of his sight. My first reaction was to be pleased that Paul seemed to want to build up a relationship with me and was not afraid to demonstrate positive feelings. I suppose it was a boost to my ego that I had been able to help Paul relax and relate to me. However, his attentions made me feel claustrophobic and crowded. I also sensed that it was not the relationship with me that Paul valued but physical contact in itself and that anyone (or at least any mother figure) would have been treated in the same way.

On Saturday night we put on a video. During the one and a half hours we spent watching it Paul lay on the settee cuddling up to me with a blanket wrapped round us. It was the only time during the weekend that Paul was quiet and at peace. This seemed much more natural than the bear hugs. It gave the impression less of disturbed but more of regressive behaviour, like that of a very young child who looks for close physical contact with his mother.

Paul's relationship with Neil during the weekend was much more distant. Although he was happy to help Neil with the gardening, he did not use this time for conversation or to instigate any physical contact such as playfighting.

When Paul went to bed on Sunday night, Neil and I spent some time reviewing the weekend. We both felt that we had made significant steps in developing our relationship with Paul. We were particularly pleased that he had stuck posters in his room, as this suggested a commitment to us or at least that Paul was prepared to try to make the placement work. We were also pleased that Paul had very quickly made moves to be physically close. We were not particularly concerned that his relationship with Neil was at a purely superficial level, because we had been told to expect this, and were not particularly perturbed by the extreme nature of Paul's behaviour, because once again we had been warned of this aspect of his personality. The fact that Paul was acting as we had expected made us feel in control of the situation and reassured us that we had been given an accurate assessment of him. We were also pleased that the routine we had established seemed to be acceptable to Paul. All things considered, we went to bed that night feeling quite positive about the future.

I do not know who was most nervous, Neil, Paul or myself, as we made our way to school on Monday morning. When we had taken Paul to see the school during the introductions he seemed to like it, chiefly because it was an attractive new building, painted in bright primary colours, not like the 'traditional' model of school to which he had been used. We had chosen this particular school not only because it was close to my mother, a practical necessity, but because we had been impressed with the headmistress who had seemed sympathetic to Paul and his problems. Another consideration was that the school had a varied catchment area and I did not think that Paul would feel out of place there. This was important, because Paul had been very aware of our status when he first met us. He thought that we were 'snobs' because we lived in a residential area and had a middle-class lifestyle. We felt that if Paul went to a school in a middle-class area he might not settle and make friends because he would see himself as different from the other children. The fact that the school was seven miles from our house, therefore making it difficult for Paul to see the other children during his leisure times, was not the disadvantage it might seem. Paul had difficulty in relating to peers and if he did not have any pressure to sustain friendships outside school it might make it easier for him to make friends in school.

What concerned Paul most was having to wear a school uniform. His earlier complaints re-emerged as we were going to school but they seemed to be token rather than serious complaints and when we arrived he went without fuss to his class. When he returned in the evening Paul reported that the school was OK. He had "got on OK" with his teachers and fellow pupils and the work had been OK. He commented that the set-up of the school was odd being divided not into separate classes but into 'bays', but again that was OK. This wonderfully informative statement was about all Paul was prepared to say before changing the subject so we had to be content with this and the knowledge that the first day had passed without any problems.

Paul had only one week of schooling before the Easter holidays and for the remainder of the week he continued to "get on OK". He was given extra attention by staff and pupils alike because he was new and spoke with a slightly different accent to the majority of the children. Paul responded positively to this special treatment. He also got on well with his nan (my mother) and did not mind having to spend time with her while Neil and I were at work. They are both fans of *Neighbours* and when I arrived to collect Paul, there they would be glued to the TV, so we could not go home until the programme was finished.

At home the pattern of behaviour established at the weekend continued. Although Paul acted in a silly manner at times, there were no major problems. He spent hours sliding downstairs and rearranging the posters in his room. He continued to demand constant attention as well as physical closeness. During his waking hours it was impossible to have a moment when Paul's presence was not felt.

Our chief difficulty, though, was adjusting to the practical demands of caring for a ten-year-old child. I had not really appreciated how exhausting this would be. Getting him ready for school meant that we had no time to relax before going to work; transporting him to and from school added considerably to our working day; and as soon as we arrived home we had to start preparing a meal at the same time as trying to give Paul our attention. Although Neil and I had previously agreed to share the tasks between us, this did not really work out as planned. Neil works shifts and on at least two nights as late as 10.30 p.m. On these nights I had the entire responsibility for Paul and was shattered by the time he went to bed.

Then Neil and I began to argue over silly, trivial things. For example, one night I returned from work to find that Paul and Neil had got home before me. Instead of making dinner, Neil had fallen asleep and left Paul to run round the house. To make matters worse, there was very little food in the freezer. I was incensed — out of all proportion — and screamed at Neil that, as usual, he was leaving all the chores and responsibilities to me. Neil was flabbergasted and could not understand why I was reacting in this way. Normally I would just have had a slight moan before getting on with the cooking or buying a take-away. Now I was so pent up that Neil falling asleep was the final straw.

Susan came to see us towards the end of that week. Her visit helped us to off-load some of our tensions and worries and to work out how to manage the situation better. We trusted Susan enough to be honest with her and knew she would not take sides or think less of us because we were admitting to having problems. By the time she left we felt much better able to cope. However, I am not sure Susan felt the same. She wrote in her case record: "Both Catherine and Neil were looking really tired. Paul was quite high and ... generally behaving in a really silly way. Neither Catherine nor Neil were particularly pulling Paul up in this."

The practical problem of not having enough food in the house was soon resolved by going out on Saturday morning to buy a month's supply of food. We filled three trolleys in the supermarket and spent £146. The freezer shop accounted for another £80. Paul loved the shopping trip, a novel experience for him. He was in his element pushing a trolley and helping to decide what to buy. He insisted on keeping the till receipts and was astounded by the amount of money we had spent.

On Sunday John returned home from university for the Easter holidays. This eased some of the remaining pressure, because he had agreed to look after Paul during his vacation. For the next two weeks we did not have to get Paul ready in the mornings — in fact he sometimes did not get up until after we had left for work — or spend time transporting him to and from school or my mother's. John also shared some of the household tasks, leaving Neil and me with only the evening routine. This gave us an excellent opportunity to get used more gradually to the work involved in being Paul's parents.

John's time at home also gave both boys an opportunity to begin to build a relationship. This went very well. Paul and John have similar personalities and this no doubt helped. I had expected them to be jealous of each other, John because he was not used to sharing my attention and Paul because he would be aware of my feelings for John and see him as a threat. This showed in their relationship with me but not with each other. John was desperate to tell me all he had been doing at university. He had recently met his first serious girlfriend and spent hours talking to me about her. Paul, at times, resented the attention John was getting and butted into our conversations. I felt torn between the two and was careful to make time when John and I could be on our own together.

The major problem between them arose because John was not sure how to handle Paul. Both boys are bright and both like to expound on a variety of topics. When Paul began to tell us anything John would elaborate, thinking he was being helpful by taking an interest in what Paul was saying and by trying to increase Paul's knowledge. In fact it left Paul feeling upstaged. His way of demonstrating his resentment was quite funny. John at the time wore a grey trench coat and Paul likened him to a bumbling detective called Inspector Gadget. He saw John as a 'know-all' who was constantly trying to show everyone that he was cleverer than Paul. When I asked John to imagine what he would feel like in Paul's place, he soon realised how his behaviour could be misinterpreted by Paul. Although John's love of sharing knowledge will always be a feature of their relationship, he did make an effort to change and even asked Paul's advice on a number of occasions. Paul loved this and I was amused to hear John asking questions and Paul earnestly explaining things which John knew perfectly well.

An incident occurred one day while Neil and I were at work which again showed that John did not always realise the implications of his actions. Apparently Paul thought it would be fun to get John into trouble. If he prevented John from tidying up the house, he reckoned I would be annoyed with John for not doing his share of the jobs. Paul spent the entire morning pestering John, stealing his books when he was trying to study, butting him and generally being a nuisance. Eventually John got fed up and put Paul out of the house. Paul responded by pouring water through the letter-box. By the time I got home the hall carpet was soaking and each boy blaming the other, John because Paul had done the damage, Paul because John had "locked him out of his own house", although he did admit to having started the quarrel. Again I felt torn in two because I could understand both points of view and was convinced I would lose if I took sides. Eventually I simply told them they were equally to blame and must both help clean up the carpet. I pointed out to Paul that 'bugging' people was not acceptable behaviour and to John that Paul had an equal right to be in the house as he had and that he should not have locked him out. In this way nobody lost face.

Towards the end of the Easter vacation we took our first family holiday — a long weekend skiing at Aviemore. A friend of mine and her nine-year old son, Keith, who I hoped would provide company for Paul, accompanied us for two of the days. It was a wonderful weekend. It was Paul's first experience of skiing and he really took to the sport. Apart from the skiing lesson I arranged for him, which he interpreted as our method of acquiring a childminder so we could go off and ski by ourselves, he thoroughly enjoyed himself. The highlight of the weekend was Sunday, a glorious day which we spent on the nursery slopes at the top of the mountain. By the afternoon conditions for skiing were perfect and we whizzed up and down the slopes with Paul singing at the top of his voice a song which he had made up especially for the occasion - "Boogy on the skis, boogy on the slopes". His happiness was infectious.

In the evening we went to the sauna and jacuzzi. Again both were new experiences for Paul but he was only too willing to try them. He particularly liked the jacuzzi which he described as a "tickly bubbles machine". Despite the fact that at times he feels little or no pain, he does seem to be particularly sensitive to sensuous experiences and loves getting his back tickled.

That day was probably the most relaxed since Paul came to stay with us and, after putting Paul and Keith to bed, the rest of us chatted about how well Paul seemed to be settling down and how well he had got on with Keith, whose life experiences were so different from those of Paul. There had been minor jealousies but nothing to cause alarm. Suddenly we became aware of raised voices. Paul was boasting about the number of Easter eggs he had and saying that he did not intend to share them. Keith took exception to this display of greed and suddenly shouted, "Well, you'd better stop being so greedy or Catherine and Neil will send you back to the orphanage they got you from". My friend, Neil and I froze. We were sure Paul would be devastated by this remark, that it would bring out all his insecurity. Instead he retorted, "It wasn't an orphanage and they can't send me back - so there". The argument was over, both boys felt they had scored a point, and they went to sleep quite amicably. I breathed a sigh of relief and once more marvelled at the ease with which Paul was able to cope with situations in which most adults, let alone children, would have felt hurt and angry.

At the end of the holiday we returned home. Neil and I went back to work, Paul to school, and John returned to university. In short we were back to 'normality'. We did not know it at that time, but the honeymoon period was over and the 'normality' we had returned to was to be one of the most difficult periods in my life.

6
HONEYMOON OVER

By the time the holiday was over I was gradually becoming more confident in my role as parent. I was certainly pleased at the progress we had made with Paul. He was a great deal more open than I had anticipated and much more ready to look for and give affection, even though this affection could take inappropriate forms, sometimes sexual, at other times almost babylike. I found both difficult to cope with. The sexual overtones were not obvious enough for me to discuss with Paul and I was therefore uncertain how to respond. As for his regressive behaviour, what concerned me was its extent. I knew that Paul had missed a great deal of mothering and I had expected him to regress a few years but not to the baby stage. I wondered if it was appropriate to let a ten-year-old act like a baby.

However, although I felt uncomfortable at Paul's behaviour I was not overwhelmed, chiefly I am sure because I had been mentally prepared beforehand. I could see that his behaviour was not really directed at me or the way I was handling him but stemmed from his previous experiences.

Paul had a remarkable ability to take things in his stride which I thought would upset him. In the beginning, for example, we tried too hard to be perfect parents and to stick to impossible routines. When we began to realise that Paul could adapt quite easily to a less strictly organised way of life than he was used to in the children's home and that what he needed more than routine was people who could handle his behaviour, we became more relaxed. Certainly, when Susan visited us after our holiday she seemed much more positive about the situation. She recorded: "They don't look so exhausted or strained and have clearly got their act much better together in trying to support each other in caring for Paul."

Indeed we found it essential in our dealings with Paul that we should act together. This did not mean that we always acted in the same way — this would have been impossible given our very different personalities — but we took care to back each other up and to adopt the same basic approach. Communication was also very important, particularly on the nights Neil was late home. I would share the events of the evening with him when he returned from work. This helped Neil feel involved with Paul even when he was not there and helped me off-load any problems. Such sharing was to prove increasingly necessary when, in the next few weeks, Paul's behaviour deteriorated.

Our return from holiday heralded the end of the 'honeymoon' period. From then on Paul started to have serious temper tantrums. Initially these tantrums only took place in the house and only when I was on my own with him. One of the first and most severe occurred on a bath night. We had been told that Paul did not enjoy baths and would often resist them. We had therefore arranged bath nights to coincide with Neil's early shifts, but this particular night Neil had had to change his shift and I decided not to disrupt Paul's routine. The evening started off fairly well. I picked Paul up from his nan's and took him home. There had been some friction when I asked Paul how he had got on at school. He replied that what happened there was the teacher's affair, not mine. I explained to Paul that parents have a responsibility for their children at all times and that what happened in school was very much my business. Paul disagreed but did not make a particular fuss. I felt his attitude illustrated his need to compartmentalise the different areas of his life, as well as his past and his present (for example, it was significant that after he came to live with us, Paul refused to visit an aunt whom he was fond of and used to see regularly).

Dinner was uneventful and we settled down to watch television. Paul was a bit 'high', jumping about and not being prepared to settle to anything. At eight o'clock I told him that I would start running his bath and at that point all hell let loose. Paul said that he did not want a bath and had no intention of taking one to please me. I pointed out that this was bath night and that I was merely asking him to do something which he had previously agreed was reasonable. He replied that he did not care and that I could not make him have a bath. I now realised that the bath was only a subsidiary issue, that Paul was making it into a major confrontation to see how I would cope with a challenge to my authority. If I gave in over this issue then Paul would feel that he could manipulate and control me. I therefore told Paul to stop his nonsense and started to run the bath.

I tried to remain calm, to act as though I was making a reasonable request which I did not see as a confrontational issue, and yet to make it clear that he was going to have a bath, like it or not.

Paul then tore round the house, in and out of the rooms. When I tried to stop him, he began to attack me, pushing me, swearing at me, kicking me. He rushed into the kitchen, grabbed a knife and told me that if I came near he would stab me. I had no option but to restrain him, so I grabbed his arm, took the knife away and pulled him on to the settee and literally sat on him. Paul responded by trying to kick, bite and punch me. I sat on his legs and held his wrists. I told him that I was not prepared to let him go until he stopped trying to hurt me and agreed to have a bath. I would hold him for ten minutes and then see if he could control himself enough to behave.

Paul struggled to get free and subjected me to a mouthful of sexually abusive language. Some of the words he used were extremely upsetting, made more so because he personalised them and because I had never heard such extreme language from a child. It was obviously designed to demoralise me and bring into question my sexual identity. I decided to ignore the language for the time being. I felt that it was more important to get the message across that he was not going to be allowed to hurt and threaten me. I also felt that it was important for Paul to know that I would never deliberately hurt him, so when he accused me of holding him too tightly I told him that I would release his hands if he agreed not to scratch or punch me. He agreed, but the moment I let him go he broke his promise. I had to grab his arms again and although I tried to be gentle with him, he continued to scream that I was hurting him. I told him that I would never deliberately do this but that if he attacked me I had to protect myself.

After ten minutes I let Paul go but again he ran round the house, throwing things at me and kicking me. Again I restrained him. This continued for about one and a half hours, at the end of which I was exhausted, my wrists were sore from trying to stop Paul from hurting me and I was beginning to wonder how much longer I could keep this up. Fortunately Paul gave in first and at ten o'clock he calmed down and agreed to have a bath. I felt utterly drained as though I had just come through a battle, but by the time he had finished his bath and put his pyjamas on, he was back to his normal self. It was as though the incident had not happened.

I poured myself a glass of wine and sank into a chair. The house was a mess. Things that Paul had thrown at me were strewn all over the place but I could not face the thought of picking them up. I was physically and mentally exhausted and for a while too tired even to think about what had happened and why. By the time Neil returned from work I was ready to talk, in a turmoil of words which reflected the turmoil which I was feeling. Simply telling my story helped me to relax and come to terms with the incident. Neil was very supportive. He praised me for remaining calm and in control by myself. His positive encouragement helped me to relax and to feel more confident.

Neil also gave me practical advice on how to restrain Paul, without hurting him, but with less effort on my part, so that during future tantrums I would be less exhausted and my wrists would not get as sore. I began to feel more in control of the situation. Perhaps I could not stop the tantrums but at least they would not have such a damaging effect on me.

Within a few days Paul was having a major tantrum every evening Neil was not at home. They would generally start off in the same way. We would get home, have dinner, then Paul would start to act in an agitated manner. Soon he would become angry and a tantrum would ensue. There was very rarely a reason for these tantrums in terms of an argument, although Paul would try to create one, perhaps using a single remark of mine as an excuse. The actual progress of the tantrum was also the same. He would start running around swearing and shouting and then become increasingly aggressive, perhaps throwing things or pushing me. He did not always pick up a knife, but when he did I never felt his threats were serious. I would try to remain calm and to reason with Paul in the hope that by not over-reacting I could help him to calm down. This never worked. The tantrums always ended with Paul trying to attack me and me having to restrain him. Neil's method of holding Paul certainly helped to reduce the physical strain on me, but although I tried very hard to be as gentle as possible with Paul, he constantly shouted that I was hurting him. I told him that I certainly did not intend to hurt him and if he did not want to risk getting hurt all he had to do was to stop the tantrums. When Neil was working at weekends the tantrums could last, on and off, for most of the day. I got some relief when I took Paul out because at that time his behaviour outside was reasonable.

I always restrained Paul for a fairly short period of time. At the end of this, I would tell him that I was going to let his arms go, that if he behaved quietly for five minutes, I would then let him go, but if not I would have to restrain him again. I would then let his arms go. Sometimes at this point he would remain calm, more often than not he would start trying to punch me. If this happened, I would go through the whole procedure again, holding him for slightly longer periods of time. Sometimes this could take hours. When he was able to lie still, I would let him go. Again this was a point of decision for Paul. Sometimes he would calm down, but more often he would immediately start rushing about the house again, and if he got the chance downstairs to his room. When I followed him he would dash under his bunk bed, grabbing a stick or some other object to hit me as he went. If I ignored him, he would come out of hiding and again start to throw things at me. The only way I could stop this was somehow to get to him and restrain him again.

Throughout all this, Paul would aim a barrage of swearing and sexually abusive language at me. The personal aspect of this left me feeling emotionally very vulnerable. Even so, I would argue that Paul's words were a minor issue in comparison to his physical attacks. By virtually ignoring his language and trying to show him that it had no effect on me, I was able to concentrate my efforts on reducing the ferocity of his attacks. Once I did not have to restrain him, I could move on to tackle the verbal abuse. I also kept reminding myself that his words were not really aimed at me personally, but were a manifestation of his very disturbed background.

One of the most disturbing features of these scenes was that throughout I felt Paul was totally in control of his behaviour and was capable of altering it at a moment's notice. I have several reasons for thinking this. First, Paul often looked as though he was enjoying the commotion and enjoying being restrained. Secondly, he would quite often stop his tantrum to watch TV or to ask a question which had nothing to do with the situation. Thirdly, he constantly asked me the time. He wanted to know how long it would be until Neil came home, because by his own admission he was afraid how Neil would respond to a tantrum and wanted to make sure it was over and he was in bed and asleep before Neil got back. He became quite skilful at timing his tantrums. Fourthly, Paul's reactions at the stages when I stopped restraining him seemed quite arbitrary. His decision whether or not to continue a tantrum had no rhyme nor reason.

We were naturally very reluctant to leave Paul with anyone. It is true he had stayed with my mother and had not caused her any serious problems; but the visit of a very close friend proved we could not be certain Paul would maintain this behaviour with other people. Before Paul came to us, Catherine used to visit me every Wednesday, staying overnight, and after the Easter holiday we decided to resume this arrangement. From the first, the atmosphere was strained. Paul obviously did not like Catherine's 'intrusion' into his house and the fact that when she was there he did not have my undivided attention. However, things went reasonably well until one Wednesday when I had to take the dog to the vet. I asked Catherine if she could keep an eye on Paul. During the half hour I was out Paul had one of his tantrums. He told Catherine to get out of the house, tried to kick her and threatened her with a knife. Catherine was so scared she locked herself into one of the rooms until I returned. It took her several hours to calm down and she did not visit me again at home for about a year.

There were some extenuating circumstances in Paul's behaviour. He was only beginning to become established in the house and Catherine's presence probably seemed like a threat. He might well not have behaved as badly in Catherine's own house. Furthermore, Catherine was also his natural mother's name, as well as mine, and he may have associated the name with the abuse he suffered as a child. But although I could rationalise Paul's reaction to Catherine as being a special case, I could not after this episode feel relaxed about leaving Paul with a childminder.

It is difficult to describe the strain Paul's behaviour imposed on me. I often felt totally drained of all energy. I dreaded going home from work when Neil would not be there and was keyed up as we drove back from my mother's as to how the evening would develop. At weekends I always hoped that he would behave reasonably for a couple of hours before the tantrum started. I have to admit that Paul rarely physically hurt me but he did considerable damage in the house. He smashed objects by hurling them at me, ruined the hall wallpaper by throwing paint over it, broke the carpet cleaner by jumping on it, to give just a few examples.

What made the whole situation more difficult to cope with was the fact that Paul seemed to choose to behave in this way. If a child cannot help what he is doing, there may be a therapeutic process by which he has to work through some of the traumas in his life. There is a possible end in sight. With Paul it was difficult for me to see any possible progression through his behaviour. He might never choose to behave any differently. Furthermore, the very idea that a child could deliberately choose to treat me so badly was very difficult to accept. I tried to be very patient and understanding in the hope that he would respond to this by wanting to behave in a different manner. He didn't! No amount of telling him that I cared about him, that I knew he could behave better, that I would continue to restrain him whenever he became aggressive, that his behaviour would not get him anywhere, had any effect on him. Later I realised that my calm and reasonable approach to his totally unreasonable behaviour was probably something Paul could not deal with. Anger would have been a 'normal' reaction which he could have understood. Now he was as powerless as myself. "What have I got to do to make her angry? what have I got to do to make her act normally?" We were therefore in a 'no win' situation which continued for several weeks.

The effect of all this on Neil's and my relationship was disastrous. We had very little time or energy for ourselves, rarely went out together as a couple, and rarely discussed anything but Paul. Often Neil would come home from work to find me tired and deflated, the house looking as though a bomb had struck it, to hear stories of yet another violent and aggressive outburst from Paul. I would describe the entire situation in great detail to Neil, but I tended to do this in a superficial way, bottling up my angry and vulnerable feelings. It was the only way I could cope with the pressure of Paul's behaviour, but this made it difficult for Neil to give me the emotional support which might have drawn us together. Instead of feeling he was playing an equal part in the situation, he could do little but sit and listen and I am sure he often felt even more worried and powerless that I did.

I used our social worker in much the same way as I used Neil. After any particularly distressing scene I would telephone Susan and this gave me the strength to face another scene. She also visited us every week. These sessions were vital because she helped us to put the negative aspects of Paul's behaviour into perspective and to make them more bearable.

Obviously there was more to Paul than tantrums and on the days when Neil was at home his behaviour was quite different. He acted more like a normal child although he was still very demanding, expecting to be the focal point in the house, with most of the conversation centring round him. If Neil and I tried to talk about our work, for example, Paul would interrupt.

At other times he acted like a much younger child, a toddler or even a baby. He would curl up on my knee or cuddle up to me in a blanket on the settee for hours. Generally I would comply with these requests, feeling that Paul would only progress and come to terms with his past if he was allowed to re-experience his baby and toddler phase in a safe environment. It was gratifying that he very quickly trusted me enough to be able to regress in this way, but it was quite tiring and emotionally draining to have Paul so physically close. I also sometimes wondered whether I was doing more harm than good by allowing him to regress so far and on one occasion I drew the line when he wanted to suck my thumb. However, despite these concerns, I was sure that Paul's regressive behaviour, unlike his tantrums, had a purpose. It also helped my relationship with him. In his softer, more obviously vulnerable moods it was hard not to feel close to him.

One odd problem about Paul which we began to suspect was that he had been urinating in a corner of the bathroom rather than in the toilet. We were not particularly surprised, because Paul had been allowed to urinate all over his parents' house. We knew that we would have to deal with this, but it was not until Paul urinated into some small ornaments in the bathroom that his behaviour was so obvious that he could not deny it. Neil explained to Paul that in our house we only urinated in the toilet. He tried to get Paul to talk about his behaviour but Paul could not verbalise his reasons. However, we felt that by explaining that his behaviour was not acceptable and giving him the opportunity to talk, we helped him realise that we understood that he did not always know how to behave and that we would not condemn him for it. So long as Paul listened, that was as much as we could expect.

Other problems were less unusual, for example Paul's poor eating habits. He had difficulty using a knife and fork and gobbled his food as quickly as possible. He was also a noisy, loud child and very careless with his belongings. He had little concern for others, being so institutionalised that he found it difficult to understand or accept family life. These were fairly minor problems, which we thought would gradually be overcome as Paul settled with us and learned how to behave, but they did add to the general tension in the house, for example at mealtimes. His endless excuses for not having baths also got on our nerves.

Often Paul's response to difficulties in the house was to threaten to run away. He would go and pack his rucksack with his bird books, spare jumper, a few toys, Garfield always peering out on top. On the first occasion I was not aware that Paul had run away until after he had returned and I found his packed rucksack on the garden path and asked Paul why it was there. Paul would always make his intentions absolutely clear: "And don't bother telling the police. They will never find me. I'll just go away and nobody will ever see me again". I invariably treated these pronouncements in a low key way, saying that I hoped he would not leave but that if he did I would have to report him as missing and he would be found and returned. Sometimes to please me Paul would agree not to leave until after he had tea or watched *Neighbours*; but he never did leave or at least never got beyond the first gate. It was sad, so desperate was he to be wanted and yet too unsure of us to risk running away in case we did not come after him. For my part, I knew I would have had a great deal of difficulty coping if he had disappeared but I was careful to keep this from Paul in case he used it against me.

Problems in school were also beginning to emerge. This was disappointing because during the first few weeks he had seemed to be settling in well, both in the classroom and outside in his relationships with his peers. Now, although he continued to cope in class, his behaviour began to deteriorate during breaks and lunch hours. On several occasions he bullied younger children, usually girls, in the playground. After four of these incidents in a fortnight, the headmistress confronted Paul and managed to reduce him to tears. We felt that this was some progress since he had previously responded with a show of unconcern and bravado. When Neil then spoke to Paul about his behaviour, again he seemed upset. Following this tentative success the school agreed to telephone us at once after any further incidents, so that we and the school could take immediate concerted action.

At this point I felt that the school was sympathetic to Paul and his problems. The headmistress was a remarkable person whose philosophy was that if a child cannot settle at school it is not the child who is the problem but the school. This attitude had a significant influence on how the other teachers treated Paul. They were pre-

49

pared to keep him in at break times and help him in various ways. This led us to hope that we could work with the school over Paul's problems. Unfortunately Paul's attitude was not so positive. His tendency to compartmentalise his life became increasingly evident in our dealings with the school. I did not realise the significance of this until we started to confront him about his behaviour there. Paul not only resented being asked about his behaviour but also had difficulty comprehending why we should be interested. He often told me it was up to the teachers to deal with things at school. I explained that as his parent I had a right to deal with all aspects of his life, and a responsibility to discuss his problems with his teachers. Obviously Paul's response was partly a defence against having to focus on his difficult behaviour in school, but I'm also sure that he genuinely did not believe we had a right to know what happened there, or responsibility to deal with it. I knew that I would have to break down this barrier if I was to have any effect on Paul's behaviour in school but it was a considerable time before Paul accepted my right as a parent to have an interest in his school life.

I would hate to give the impression that this period was totally negative. That was not the case. Even during the most difficult times Paul's personality and sense of humour showed. (In the throes of his worst tantrums, his insults could have their funny side — the ultimate insult, "You're nothing but a Munro bagger".) Paul laughed a great deal and got such pleasure from small things that it was impossible not to share his enjoyment. He has a creative imagination and loves knowledge. This meant that he eagerly lapped up any experiences we offered him; for instance both Neil and I are interested in birdwatching and were keen to involve Paul. He readily agreed and we made several visits to a local bird sanctuary. Paul loved looking through the binoculars and soon began to identify some of the more common birds. We bought him his own bird book and he poured over this most nights ticking off the birds he had spotted. He would spend ages drawing them and telling us about their winter habitat, number of eggs, etc. It was lovely to see him taking such an interest.

Paul's eagerness to embrace new experiences gave me the opportunity to appreciate anew some things which I was perhaps beginning to take for granted. This was particularly evident when I took him hillwalking. The first trip was with my hillwalking club to one of the hills near Glencoe. Even during the three-hour climb his eagerness did not wane. He made a considerable effort to keep up with the rest of the party (mostly adults) and to chat to them. I felt so proud of him when he finally got to the top.

Our second trip was a weekend one to Glen Sheil. Our rooms had been double booked and the best the manager could offer us was a mattress in the storeroom behind the bar. I thought that Paul would be appalled at this, but instead he joked about it. Once again he made a mammoth effort and managed to climb six Munros (mountains) on the Saturday, although he did have to give up on the second day. Paul and I both remember the weekend with plea-sure. He greatly appreciated the scenery and the atmosphere on the hills, and we ended up with several 'additions' to the family in the form of frogs which, according to Paul, "must have jumped into my kagoul pocket when I was not looking".

The most positive aspect of Paul was his loving nature. This helped to compensate for the tantrums. He could give affection as well as receive it. Once, for example, when I was putting him to bed, he asked me if he could write down something he was too embar-rassed to say. After a few minutes he passed me a folded up piece of paper. I opened it and read, "Dear Mum - when you are out at night and come home after I am in bed, do you sometimes come in and give me a wee kiss? Please write your answer below". It was so sweet and epitomised his insecurity. I was touched that he should share his feelings with me.

Even so, I have to admit that the first few weeks after the Easter holidays were very difficult. The increasing tension between Neil and myself was exacerbated by the fact that Paul kept Neil at arm's length and would only relate to him on a superficial level. I began to resent the fact that I had to deal with all the difficulties, while Neil began to feel that he was being excluded from Paul's and my relationship and blamed me for being too lenient. I felt that Neil did not fully appreciate what I had to put up with and could have tried harder to relate to Paul.

All of this came to a head about four weeks after the 'honeymoon' period. I had had a particularly stressful time. I even dreaded the thought of going to work, whereas usually I saw work almost as a relief from Paul and the pressures at home. I was becoming so tense I felt sick. I just did not know how I could go on. Fortunately Neil realised I needed a complete break and arranged to take Paul away on a fishing trip. I had a wonderfully therapeutic weekend. I drove to Fort William to stay with a friend, but was so exhausted that I could hardly talk to her and took off for a walk in the hills by myself. When I got back, my friend noticed a significant improvement in me and by Sunday I was able to look forward to meeting Neil and Paul. It was good to see them again and to tease them about the fact that they had not managed to catch a single fish.

I realised, though, how important it is to know when things are getting too much and to take a break from the pressures, even if only for a few hours. My means of escape is to go off into the hills for the day. It is vital that other adoptive parents work out their own method of relaxing.

7
DISCLOSURES

Nothing changed after my weekend away except my resolve to do something positive about Paul's tantrums. Susan had stressed that Paul should be getting a clear message that he was not going to be allowed to behave as he had. She felt that I was almost giving him permission to have a tantrum by not intervening more positively. I agreed with Susan and, although I could not think of any more effective ways of deflecting the tantrums than those I had previously tried, I was determined that at least I should not allow Paul totally to control the pace and timing of his tantrums.

Meanwhile Paul's behaviour at school had escalated to such a level that we were telephoning the teachers every day to check how he had behaved. On the Thursday following the weekend away Paul hit out at a five-year-old girl in the playground. I discussed the incident with the school and agreed that for a while Paul should be kept in during playtime and lunch breaks. I confronted Paul about his behaviour on the way back home in the car. He deeply resented me talking to him about the incident and the fact that I had agreed that he should be kept in during breaks.

When we arrived home Paul started poking me, saying that he had a right to 'bug' me because I had been 'bugging' him. I tried to dismiss this because I was cooking and wanted to get the evening meal over with before focusing on Paul, but his behaviour became more and more extreme. He threatened me with a screwdriver and when I took it away from him, he began to run around the house. At dinner he behaved almost like an animal, grabbing the food with his hands and trying to cram two whole tomatoes into his mouth at the same time. When I remonstrated with him he threw the remainder of his dinner at me. When I tried to hold him he put the dog's collar round my neck and then bit and kicked me. I responded by smacking Paul once on the leg, fairly gently and not in anger, although to be honest without much thought of the possible consequences. Paul's behaviour changed dramatically. He completely lost control. He became hysterical, rushed behind the couch and hid under a blanket screaming, "Don't hit me, don't hit me". He was like a frightened animal cowering in a corner. His terror was apparent. I was horrified. Paul's behaviour communicated such panic and fear that he made me realise, in a way which the reports had not, the traumas he had suffered as a younger child and to understand to some extent what it had been like for him when he lived with his natural family. (Paul's ability to convey his feelings was something both his psychologist and Julie had noted.) I felt sick and shaken. I knew his response was totally out of all proportion to the situation and that I had not physically hurt him, but this did not make me feel any less guilty. I should have known better than to resurrect the abuse Paul had suffered from his natural parents.

To approach Paul when he became so hysterical would only have increased his hysteria and fear. Instead I stayed fairly near him and tried to reassure him by saying that he would not get hurt by me, that the rules in this house were different from those in his natural parents' home. He calmed down after a while and to my surprise resumed his former temper tantrum, although with a difference. For the first time, he interspersed his swearing with expressions such as "You don't really care about me" and "Why don't you send me back?". Was this a testing out of our feelings and the beginning of a commitment to living with us? I decided that this was not a time to restrain Paul, in case it brought back his terror. However, I would not let the tantrum continue unabated. I therefore telephoned Neil at his work and he returned home and took over. As soon as he came into the house Paul calmed down and rushed to his bed. Neil made it clear to Paul that his behaviour was unacceptable and asked him why he never had tantrums when he was there. Paul managed to explain that he was afraid that if he had a tantrum with Neil, Neil might resort to hurting him. We used this opportunity to reiterate the message that he would not get hurt in our home, but neither would we allow him to hurt other people.

In retrospect, I feel that some good came out of this particularly traumatic scene. I now knew that I could intervene in Paul's tantrums and influence their course. I hoped that in future I could do this in a more positive way. And, very important, for the first time Paul had been able by his actions to demonstrate his true feelings. I hoped that before long he would feel able to share his experiences in words.

The following day when I telephoned Susan I thought that she might be annoyed that I had smacked Paul, but she focused more on the positive aspects of the situation as well as the fact that Paul could have hurt me. She suggested that I should show anger at Paul's behaviour, even if I did not feel it, to re-enforce the message that tantrums would not be tolerated. Words might not be enough. The evening might have developed differently if, as soon as Paul started poking at me, I had physically restrained him and made him talk through his feelings of anger rather than act them out. I had been thinking along the same lines and was determined that immediately the next tantrum began I would intervene by becoming angry and restraining Paul. I would also tell Paul exactly what I was doing because I felt that part of the reason for his extreme reaction to my smack was because it came totally out of the blue and was quite out of character.

I got the opportunity to try out my new techniques a few days later when Neil was next on a late shift. Shortly after Paul and I came home he began to run around and to poke at me. My show of anger had little effect, but by restraining Paul at once and continuing to restrain him I managed to reduce the build up to the tantrum considerably and we had a relatively calm end to the day. The tantrum itself had, it was true, been quite severe and had lasted two hours, but at least that was no longer than average, and the build up was much less than the usual one to two hours. This was the first bit of progress I had made. I felt I was beginning to have some control over the situation. The next stage would be to reduce the length of the actual tantrum.

A little progress was also made at school, but only after an incident when Paul went completely berserk and lashed out at another child. The teachers did not know how to calm the situation and so removed him from the classroom and kept him on his own for the remainder of the day. We knew the school would not continue to accept this sort of behaviour and we felt drastic measures were called for. We had decided that Neil would deal with the school issue, partly because he had more control over Paul and partly because I had enough to contend with at home. We were sure one of the reasons for Paul's difficulties at school was that he preferred to be at home. He knew that the school's major disciplinary tactic was suspension, so by misbehaving he could get what he wanted. Paul's commitment to school might be increased if we made the alternatives less pleasant. The following day, luckily, was a holiday at Paul's school and Neil was granted permission to take Paul into the residential school where he works. We told Paul that he could make up for his misbehaviour at his own school by attending his dad's school on his holiday. Paul was quite upset and apprehensive about going to a residential school but he went with Neil without complaint. He spent most of the day sitting in a room with school-work and we were pleased when he said that he had disliked his dad's school and would not like to go back there. We hoped that this would act as a deterrent to bad behaviour and certainly for the next week or so it seemed effective. We were able to cut down our calls to his teachers from every day to two or three times a week.

However, there were two major areas where progress had not been made. One of these was Paul's attitude to our cat and dog. When he had first been introduced to our pets he had taken an affectionate interest in them and, as we had been assured, showed no signs of cruelty. He enjoyed taking our dog, Bonzo, for a walk and loved the attention they received when they were out together (Bonzo is an unusual breed and people often stop to admire him.) But then Paul's attitude to both animals began to change. I think he felt threatened by them because they had been in the house before he arrived and because he realised that Neil and I were fond of them. There is no doubt he was jealous of Purrball (our cat) and Bonzo and he showed this by deliberately trying to hurt them. With Bonzo Paul got no resistance — he is very docile and would merely whimper — but Purrball would retaliate by hissing at Paul and scratching him. Paul deeply resented this, and could not see that he had only himself to blame.

The feud culminated one night when Paul sprayed the cat with a cleaning fluid. I heard Purrball choking and found him cowering in a corner foaming at the mouth, with his fur all slicked down and wet. Panic stricken, I shouted for Neil who immediately realised what had happened. He grabbed Purrball and poured gallons of water over the terrified animal in order to wash the stuff out of his fur to stop him from licking and poisoning himself. It was about half an hour before Purrball was almost back to normal and before we had time even to think about Paul. We then discovered that he had left the house; probably he had heard me shouting. Although he was not far away we made no attempt to call him. We knew that he would be worried at our reaction and scared we might reject him. Neither Neil nor I were inclined to assuage these feelings. We felt that it would be good for Paul to realise how angry we were with him and that feelings of rejection might bring home to him how seriously we took his actions. Paul gradually moved closer to the house and made more obvious attempts to attract our attention but again we ignored him. Eventually he knocked at the door and we let him in. I told him how angry I was that he had hurt the cat, that he could have poisoned Purrball, and that I wanted nothing more to do with him for that night. Paul spent the remainder of the evening until bedtime trying in vain to engage me in conversation and to win me over. The fact that I did not respond seemed to have a profound effect on him.

The second major problem was Paul's increasingly quasi-sexual manner towards me. I sensed this not so much in what he did as in the feeling and intent behind his actions. Often it was obvious that his enjoyment of kisses and cuddles was a manifestation of his regression to babyhood. However, at other times, these kisses and cuddles seemed to have a sexual element and I was aware of very small changes in the way he approached me and looked at me. One night, for example, Paul had been sitting on the settee cuddling up to me watching television. This seemed perfectly natural and normal. After a while he moved a bit closer, placed his hand upon my breast and looked at me to see my response. In the past Paul had cuddled up to me with his hands near my breast without there being any sexual overtones, but the deliberate way in which he acted on this occasion made me feel uncomfortable. I was very conscious of his hand on my breast and felt I was being sexually exploited. I did not know what to do. Should I ignore it, pretending that nothing was wrong? Paul might interpret this as condoning sexual contact between us. Or should I make it clear to Paul that this way of touching was not appropriate? But I was not sure I would be able to make Paul grasp the difference between appropriate and inappropriate kisses and cuddles, and I did not want to do anything which would make Paul feel that he should not show affection. In the event I did neither. I merely made an excuse to get up, thereby getting myself out of the situation without having to confront Paul. There were many other similar, but not often such obvious, situations to which I responded in the same way.

I knew that this response was not helping Paul and that I ought to raise the issue of his sexual behaviour with him. When I consulted

Susan she immediately appreciated the situation and reassured me that many foster and adoptive parents reported similar problems with children who had been sexually abused. She said I should be more confident about the validity of my feelings and should give Paul clear messages about what was and what was not acceptable behaviour. She thought Paul would know exactly what I meant, but that I would have to show him, not just tell him, what was not acceptable. She recommended a video by Vera Fahlberg. [1] I watched this and it certainly gave me confidence as well as practical advice. I would certainly recommend it to anyone who fosters or adopts such a child.

For the next week or so Paul's behaviour continued to be very difficult, alternating between tantrums and extreme affection. There was virtually no time when I could describe Paul's behaviour towards me as that of a normal child. However, I did not feel quite as hopeless as before. When Paul started the build up to a tantrum, I intervened immediately. Gradually the timescale of the tantrums changed. Sometimes Paul did not have one until later at night, or if he had one earlier he nearly always finished it well before bedtime. Most nights we had some time together when Paul's behaviour was if not normal at least a great deal more positive.

After Paul had been with us for about two and a half months, there was something of a breakthrough. The night had started off fairly normally, if anything Paul's behaviour had been better than usual. About 8.45 p.m he decided that he was going to have a tantrum. This followed the usual course except that on this occasion when Paul refused to get ready for bed I partly undressed him and put his pyjamas on. Paul became hysterical and wild, his breathing panicky and shallow. I made him sit down on the settee and asked him to tell me why he was behaving like this. Paul said that it was none of my business and that he had no intention of telling me. I told him that his tantrums upset me considerably and that therefore it was my business. I was prepared to sit there all night if necessary until he told me why he was behaving so badly. For a while there was a stalemate. Eventually Paul said that he would tell me if I let him get into bed. I agreed. Paul got into bed, lay down and said goodnight. I reminded him that this was not the deal. We then went through

---

[1] A list of materials produced by Vera Fahlberg is available from Ms Fahlberg, Forest Heights Lodge, Evergreen, Colorado, USA.

another see-saw of "I'm not telling", "I'm waiting here until you do". Paul told me that I was wasting my time, that I must have many more things to do. I answered that I had nothing more important to do and that I had all the time in the world for him. I wanted to emphasise that Paul was important to me and that anything he said would be treated as important.

I suggested that, if it was too difficult for him to start the conversation, I would put forward possible reasons for his behaviour and he could tell me if these were correct. Paul seemed quite pleased to be helped. I suggested that because he had always been allowed to behave badly he thought he could so the same in our house. Paul denied this. I wondered whether he was beginning to enjoy staying with us and whether a tantrum was a bit of a dare. Paul said that was partly true, but the main reason that he hurt me was to pay his parents back for all the times they had hurt him. When I asked him if he wanted to talk about this, he said he would like to but then seemed uncertain how to start. To encourage him I said that I knew his mum used to hit him, that she locked him in a cupboard, that he did not always have enough to eat. Paul acknowledged that these things had happened to him. I said that I thought his dad had been better towards him but Paul denied this. Both were equally bad. Paul then went on to say that I did not know all that had happened and, when I agreed with this, he described how his parents beat him with a belt and threw things at him. I asked Paul if he could remember any good things in his house. He said no, only bad things. I told Paul that I was very sorry that these things had happened to him but that I could not undo them. I hoped that as he settled with us he would build up some happy memories of our home which would diminish the importance of the bad things that happened when he was living with his natural parents and might help him remember some of the good things. It seemed important that Paul should realise that his past was made up of both positive and negative experiences. Also, I did not want him to feel that he had to deny the good bits about his parents in order to be accepted by me.

I led the conversation back to the reasons why he had tantrums. I said that I could understand why Paul wanted to pay his parents back, but by hurting me he was not achieving his objective. He had been unhappy much of the time with his parents, but what was the point of making himself unhappy now by having tantrums and being restrained? If he really wanted to pay his parents back, why not behave reasonably and therefore allow me to treat him in a way that would make him happy? I also told Paul that I would never treat him as his natural mother had done. But I also made it clear that I could not continue to let him have tantrums. I knew that he was capable of behaving better and gave him examples of ways in which he had improved. If he was angry he should talk to me about how he felt rather than have a tantrum.

The whole scene had lasted over two hours and by the time Paul settled down for the night I was both physically and emotionally exhausted. I could not wait to tell Neil about the events of the evening. Yet, despite my exhaustion, I felt pleased. For the first time Paul had been able to share some of his feelings about his past with me. This helped put the first two and a half months into perspective. I had previously thought that most of his destructive and aggressive behaviour was aimed at testing out whether we were prepared to accept the worst parts of him. I now realised that at this stage Paul did not care enough about us to want to test out our commitment to him. While retribution helped to explain why his behaviour had seemed so pointless, I wondered whether there was more to it than that. Had Paul, perhaps subconsciously, been trying to place himself in the role of the aggressor, his mother's role, to see if I had the power to control his aggression and protect him from his mother? Only then would he be able to look to me for protection and security. But whatever the explanations I felt that significant progress had been made.

However, I had to question my own handling of the situation. First, was I right to force Paul to talk about his background and feelings? On balance I think I was and that he could have avoided opening out to me if he had not wanted to. But I would acknowledge that this approach might not always be appropriate. Second, should I have told Paul that I knew about the sexual abuse? Neil thought that I should, that I had wasted a good opportunity. My justification was that I did not want to push Paul into revealing the sexual abuse until he was ready, but I knew I would find the revelations difficult to cope with. Susan thought that there would be other opportunities. In fact the first disclosure occurred the next day.

I had been quite disappointed during the early part of the evening, because Paul had yet another tantrum. I had hoped for at least a few days' peace and quiet. However, this particular tantrum turned out to have a purpose because Paul used it to set the scene for his disclosure. I was to discover, as time progressed, that Paul had to work up to some sort of crisis before he could discuss any important issues.

Paul's mood continued until bedtime. When I had given him his goodnight kiss, Paul asked if he could talk to me for a minute and handed me Garfield saying that he did not want him any more and would I take the teddy to my bed. Immediately I knew that he was going to talk to me about something important, because Paul used Garfield as his *alter ego*, blaming him for anything which got broken or went wrong. My immediate reaction was that I was too tired and that it was too late to cope with the disclosure which I knew would follow, but instead I said I would be pleased to take Garfield and asked if he wanted to tell me why he was giving me his teddy. Paul said he did want to tell me something. At first he began to talk about the physical abuse that he experienced, being locked up and hit. He said that he had told his mum to "fuck off" and that he had once tried to stab her. But I knew that this was only a lead-up to something more important. I therefore encouraged him to continue talking and eventually he told me that he had something else to tell me, but that he did not know how and whether I would hate him. I reassured Paul that I would care about him no matter what he said and had every confidence in his ability to put his feelings into words. For the next twenty minutes or so Paul continued to alternate between wanting to tell me and saying he could not do so. I remained calm (at least outwardly). He asked me whom I would share our conversation with and when I told him I would discuss it with Neil, he accepted this.

Eventually, Paul said that I must be getting tired and would I like to get into bed beside him. I did this and he then asked if he could talk to me under the covers. I replied that if he felt more comfortable there that was all right by me. Paul then pulled the bed clothes over himself and started to talk to me about his mother's sexual abuse of him. As he talked a hand came out from underneath for me to hold. Although he could not look at me, I think he needed to feel that I was close to him, that I was not rejecting him. Paul described incidents of sexual abuse in which his mother had encouraged him to have intercourse with her. This occurred about twice a week and took place over a number of years. His mother would get him to touch her breasts and other parts of her body and she would touch his penis and "balls". He described this as his mother "raping" him. He talked about his father watching while this was going on and also of instances where he was made to watch while his parents had intercourse. As he talked Paul continued to be agitated, jumping around under the covers. At one point he looked at me and said that he could see in my face that I did not love him any more. I reassured him that I did love him and I was glad that he had been brave enough to confide in me. What he saw in my face was my sadness that these things had happened to him. Paul accepted this. My role throughout was to listen and this seemed to meet his needs. I did ask a few encouraging questions, but I put no pressure on him for details because I did not want him to disclose more than he was prepared to do and because detailed questioning might have made him feel that I disbelieved him. Towards the end I asked Paul if he could remember any good bits about the abuse. Immediately he said that all he could remember was that it had been painful. I told him that, even if he had enjoyed any of it and wanted to tell me, that would not make me love him any less. By saying this, I hoped Paul would feel free to talk about the abuse again if he wished to do so.

As soon as Neil arrived home from work I rushed to tell him what Paul had disclosed. As I spoke I felt sick, anxious and agitated. I could hardly look at Neil and wanted to hide away, just as Paul had done. This brought home to me just how difficult it must have been for Paul to tell me what had happened to him. By the time I had finished I felt numb and cold inside. Neil tried to offer me comfort and support but, at that time, all I wanted to do was to distance myself from him.

The following morning Paul got up and went to school as though nothing had happened, his only reference to the previous evening being to make sure that I had taken Garfield to bed with me (which I had) and to tell me that he had been very generous to give me Garfield. He had indeed been generous, in trusting me enough to share with me some of his worst experiences.

Susan was not there when I telephoned but I spoke to her boss, Mary, who helped me relax. She was pleased that Paul had been able to talk to me, but suggested this might only be the beginning. Now Paul was only telling me facts. He would need to move on to how he felt about himself. This might mean him going over the sexual abuse many times and she assured me of her agency's support.

I would love to report that Paul's behaviour improved after this.

Unfortunately, if anything he became worse. However, although the tantrums continued unabated there did seem to be a turning point in that they became less an acting out of past experiences and more a testing out of our commitment to him. He would shout that he knew we did not want him and that he would act so badly, even smash all the windows, that we would have to send him back to the children's home. I replied, first, that I would not let him smash all the windows (confirming that we could control him); secondly, that if he did, then we would just have to live in a drafty house until we could afford to get the windows repaired (confirming that there was nothing he could do to make us reject him); and thirdly that his only real choice was whether to behave and be relatively happy or to misbehave and be unhappy (confirming that he could behave and could change the situation). It was a considerable time, though, before Paul began to accept the validity of these messages.

Even the loving aspect of Paul's behaviour became more difficult to cope with. His feelings of insecurity intensified and he was terrified that we really would reject him. He would spend literally hours sitting on my knee, cuddling me and telling me that he loved me. He would not settle until I told him that I loved him and in an almost manic way he would get me to repeat this time after time.

Paul's sexual behaviour also became more pronounced. The provocative way he touched me and moved against me was extremely distressing, but the video Susan had recommended gave me the confidence to tackle the problem. I accepted that Paul knew what he was doing and I was quite direct with him. When he touched me in a sexual manner I told him I could not let him do this and that I would have to get up for a while. I explained that it was acceptable to touch my arm but unacceptable to touch my breasts and that if he could not behave properly I would get up again. I used to do housework to distance myself from Paul. Neil always knew when Paul had been behaving sexually towards me because the dishes were done and the carpets clean!

A new development, and a particularly difficult one, was that Paul started to have tantrums outside the house. Previously I could virtually guarantee that if I took Paul out he would behave in a reasonable manner. Now there was no such break for me from Paul's tantrums, but my major concern was that the presence of other people affected my handling of the situation. Paul's behaviour was, it is true, never as bad outside as it was at home. Sometimes the tantrums amounted to little more than swearing in a shop, but on occasions his behaviour reached such a peak that I had to grab him and put his arms behind his back and march him through the town, Paul trying to attack me and subjecting me to a barrage of abusive language all the way. Passers-by saw an abusive child being dramatically restrained. Some, I'm sure, thought Paul's behaviour was disgraceful, some that it must be my fault, and others that it was I who was being abusive to Paul. These scenes were acutely embarrassing. I had an overwhelming urge to explain to my 'audience' that Paul was a very difficult and disturbed child who had only recently come to live with me and that his behaviour was neither my fault nor his. I was also concerned, I have to admit, that some of the onlookers might know my mother or know me in my work capacity. Not all foster or adoptive children behave in such an extreme manner in public, but many do behave embarrassingly. It is therefore important for the adults with them to be prepared. At the very least a thick skin is required.

Meanwhile, Paul's constant threats to run away continued, as did his jealousy of our cat and dog. This showed itself in some weird behaviour. Paul would crawl round the house pretending to be a dog, barking, panting and asking me if I would pat him and allow him to beg for biscuits. At other times he attributed almost human characteristics to Bonzo and Purrball and felt that if they did not respond positively to excessive affection they were rejecting him.

On the positive side Paul continued to display a remarkable perception well beyond his years, together with his sense of humour and his thirst for knowledge. As well as birdwatching and hillwalking, we joined the local Kayak Club. This was a mark of Paul's self-confidence because he had chosen this particular sport himself and was soon able to canoe much better than I could.

I was also encouraged by two positive events. The first occurred on a Saturday morning in the village where we live. Paul had been playing on his skateboard while I was in a shop and some older boys had taken it from him. When I came out I told them to return the skateboard immediately. Paul was proud that I was prepared to stand up for him. He told me that he was just waiting for me to "sort things out".

The second event was Sports Day. Paul had been coping fairly well at school and so was allowed to take part. I had taken the afternoon off work to attend and had bought him a matching T-shirt and shorts as well as a tracksuit. Paul looked splendid in his new clothes and was really happy. Teachers and pupils alike told him how nice he looked. This must have been particularly important to Paul who had been ostracised because of his unkempt appearance when he lived with his parents. He lapped up the attention he received and was obviously delighted by the fact that, probably for the first time ever, someone attended Sports Day exclusively to cheer him on. Coupled with this was the fact that he won a silver and gold in his races. Paul was overjoyed at my pride in his achievements and, although he pretended otherwise, his face showed how important that day had been for him.

Paul had now been with us three and a half months and had completed one full term at school. Towards the end of this period a review was held to look at the progress, both positive and negative, Paul had made since he came to stay with us. This involved the local authority, the adoption agency, the school and ourselves. Everyone at the meeting agreed that significant progress had been made. His psychologist felt that Paul had coped well with the move and showed signs of settling. She was particularly pleased by Paul's disclosure of sexual abuse as this indicated that he was beginning to build up trust in us. However, the review agreed that Paul would continue to need her support for some time. But for Neil and myself the most important support came from the adoption agency. The review confirmed that this be available for as long as we needed it and after we had adopted Paul. The fact that we did not have to choose between adopting Paul and receiving support in dealing with him helped us to come to a decision about when to apply for adoption. Although the social work staff at the review assured us that there was no pressure to proceed, I felt it would be in Paul's best interests to do so. It would give him confirmation that we had a long-term commitment to him. His previous placement with foster parents had broken down after a year or so, and I wanted Paul to know that this would not happen with us. We therefore decided to push ahead with the Adoption Petition as soon as possible.

8
SUMMER HOLIDAYS

I had been looking forward to the summer holidays for a number of reasons. I hoped that, without the pressure of worrying about whether Paul was getting into trouble at school, we might all be more relaxed. I had arranged for Paul to be looked after by my mother when Neil and I were at work and, knowing that Paul had a good relationship with his nan, I hoped that he would enjoy being with her and begin to build up some commitment to our wider family. Neil's shifts meant that he could spend more time with Paul during the day and I hoped a more positive relationship between Neil and Paul would develop as a result. We had arranged a couple of holidays with Paul which I hoped would give us the opportunity to enjoy being together as a family, while a break from work would be a rest for me. As it transpired none of these hopes were fully realised.

The first holiday, at the beginning of Paul's summer vacation, involved six of us spending a week on a boat on the Caledonian Canal — Neil and myself, John and his girlfriend Margaret, Paul, and Keith as a companion for him. John and Margaret had arrived home a few days earlier and at once problems started to emerge. Paul was jealous of both John and Margaret. He continually annoyed them and had several tantrums. I hoped that the holiday would blow away some of the tension.

Certainly the first day of the holiday made me feel that my optimism was justified. Neil and the two boys had gone ahead and by the time the rest of us arrived Paul and Keith had really taken to being sailors. They were keen to show me that they knew how to tie up the boat and helped us landlubbers transport our belongings from the shore. The boys were obviously excited at the prospect of spending a week on the boat and they vied with each other to be helpful and show off their seafaring skills. We had good fun that night and when we had to moor out in Loch Ness and paddle to the shore in a dinghy, Paul blossomed. He and John took charge of getting everyone on to the shore dry and when we returned to the boat after dinner, Paul put on his swimming trunks and paddled around in the dinghy keeping us entertained.

However, despite several such happy experiences — including unsuccessful but hilarious attempts at snorkelling — I could not describe the holiday as either positive or relaxing. It was probably not a good idea to have six people who do not all know each other well crammed into a confined space for hours on end. There was bound to be friction. But the biggest problem was Paul's behaviour. After the first night Paul spent almost the entire holiday pestering me. I could not move an inch but he was beside me. He could not bear me paying attention to anyone or anything else. He spent hours every day sitting on my knee, kissing me and cuddling me in an extremely inappropriate manner. He did this regardless of who else was present and even though I often tried to push him away. He kept telling me that I did not need Neil, that he, Paul, could be my boyfriend. He "wanted to have it off" with me. The fact that other people were present made it more difficult for me to have a frank discussion with Paul, which is probably why his behaviour persisted at such an intense level for so long. I could not explain to him in front of John, Margaret and Keith that, even if his mother had "had it off" with him, this did not make it an acceptable way to behave with me.

Paul's sexual behaviour inevitably created trouble between Neil and me. Neil thought that I was not being strict enough and was virtually condoning and almost encouraging Paul, and I was angry with Neil for not doing more to help. In several heated arguments I pointed out that he had seen what was happening and could have stepped in and taken Paul away from me. Neil disagreed. Given that the problem was between Paul and me then I should be able to tackle it. My feeling was that Neil was opting out, that he was having difficulty himself coping with this aspect of Paul. He always stepped in to deal with Paul's aggression and I could not see the difference. Both types of behaviour were inappropriate and both needed firm handling which I could not do on my own.

Paul was also aggressive and violent during the holiday, although at a reduced level than before. There was, however, one major outburst during which Paul punched me in the face and caused my nose to bleed. Neil immediately took over and restrained Paul, while John and Margaret, who had been present during the scene, calmed me down. I was extremely upset and my nose was still swollen and bruised several days later. In particular I did not want my mother to see me like that. On a previous occasion when Paul had hit me and bruised my face, I had told her that I had had a fall. I knew she would have been upset had she known the truth. Even then she had looked doubtful and I knew she would not believe a second 'fall'. I avoided visiting her after the holiday until the swelling had disappeared and told other people I had had an accident. This lying made me feel very defensive, I suppose in the way battered wives must feel when they explain away the bruises and injuries inflicted by husbands.

The holiday must have been difficult for everyone. Keith was probably least affected, but I later found out from his mother that, although he thoroughly enjoyed his holiday, he was upset by Paul's behaviour towards me. Keith is very fond of me and he did not like the way Paul swore at me and hit me. I do not think he fully appreciated the sexual overtones of much of Paul's behaviour but he certainly thought it odd to say the least. He felt that as Neil and I were offering Paul a home, Paul should be more grateful. He saw things as a child, in black and white, and could not understand that Paul's background would influence his present behaviour.

Margaret probably understood better the reasons for the tantrums. John had explained something about Paul's background, but not about the sexual abuse. She must have been aware of the sexual nature of Paul's behaviour to me and perplexed by it. I'm sure she wondered what she had let herself in for by coming on this holiday. She was certainly extremely embarrassed being with us when Paul misbehaved in public.

Although John knew much more about Paul, he was very upset and angry at having to watch him attacking me. What probably made it more difficult was that, in deference to my wishes, John never intervened or said anything directly to Paul about his behaviour. He must also have felt concerned about Margaret's feelings.

Paul I am sure, was utterly confused. He had spent the past three and a half months being with Neil and me on his own, used to our full attention, and here he was stuck on a boat having to share us with three other people. To make matters worse, he had been looking forward to this holiday. After all, he had been told that we had chosen one we thought he would particularly enjoy. Given this, his behaviour was not altogether surprising. Paul was desperate to keep my attention and the only approach he knew was sexual, the way his mother had shown him of gaining attention. When he discovered this was not effective his frustration and fear gave way to tantrums and swearing. He could not accept it when I told him that parents and children ought not to behave sexually towards each other, because his own experience showed him that they did. The fact that I could not discuss this issue with him openly only confused him further. I also feel that Neil's lack of action did nothing to confirm to Paul how inappropriate his sexual behaviour was.

Neil's difficulty in coping with Paul's behaviour was, I think, complicated by jealousy when Paul began to fawn all over me. His affection for Paul clearly took second place to his affection for me and it must have been difficult for him to see how upset and tired Paul made me and at the same time to accept how much Paul meant to me. He felt angry with Paul, and with me for tolerating Paul's behaviour, although he had considerable sympathy for me too. As a result he felt alienated from Paul and me.

As for myself, I felt isolated, as though I had been left to deal with Paul on my own. I was completely wrapped up in the immediacy of the situation and did not consider that anyone else had a role to play or an emotion to feel. After all, they were not the butt of Paul's actions. I felt very angry with Neil for not doing enough but, strangely, little or no anger towards Paul, although I often thought I would scream if he did not leave me alone. When I pushed him away I felt guilty that I was not able to cope with him in a way which did not reject him. By the end of the holiday I had never been more glad to get back to work so as to have a break from Paul's constant demands.

On returning home I immediately telephoned the adoption agency for advice. Susan was on holiday, so Mary listened to my tale. She was most sympathetic, but tried to make me see how difficult it must have been for Neil, too, to cope. I began to recognise that I was not the only person affected by Paul's behaviour. She agreed, though, that Neil should be taking a more active role in helping me.

By way of practical advice, Mary first stressed that I must consistently make it clear to Paul what was and what was not appropriate behaviour between mother and son and that I should do this regardless of who else was present. Reference to Paul's background was not necessary. In fact, explanations might not help Paul, since he

70

did not seem to be operating at a rational level but more on the level of a two-year-old. A consistent message was more important than reasons. Secondly, Mary advised me to limit the opportunities for Paul to behave sexually. I should try to ensure that he did not have long periods in close contact with me, even in the presence of others. Paul should be encouraged to find alternative occupations, possibly with Neil's help. It was obvious Paul did not know how to relate to me, how to obtain my affection without going overboard. Mary also felt he had difficulty in accepting that I could love anyone else. Only if my love were exclusively directed towards him, could he be sure that I would not reject him in favour of Neil. Paul needed to learn that I could love more than one person, without loving either less, just as he had to learn the difference between adult-child and adult-adult relationships. In short he had to learn about normal family relationships; but Mary emphasised this would take time.

I then discussed Mary's recommendations with Neil. As his work shifts made it difficult for me to minimise the opportunity for Paul to behave inappropriately, we agreed that as far as possible I would spend the evenings I had alone with Paul doing things like canoeing and swimming as opposed to aimlessly watching television. Neil also agreed to talk to Paul directly about his behaviour during the holiday, and he took a day off work to do this. Neil spoke extremely sensitively but seriously, and although Paul did not respond Neil felt that he had got the message across. He was right. That night there was a marked improvement in Paul's behaviour. He was much more relaxed with me and was able to sit by me on the settee without pawing me. However, at bedtime when I went to kiss him goodnight he told me that he was not allowed to kiss me. His dad had told him so. I had to explain, yet again, the sort of kisses he was not permitted to give me.

The following morning, Paul hid my car keys. I realised that he did not want me to go to work, that he wanted to have me to himself that day instead of going to his nan's. I told Paul I intended to work and I telephoned Neil, who was on early shift, to ask him for his spare set of keys. Paul then 'found' my keys, and I took him to my mother's and went to work. I felt that it was vitally important to show Paul that loving someone does not mean denying everyone and everything else. He did not have to take me over totally to ensure that I cared.

That night I decided to talk to Paul about the morning's incident and about his recent behaviour, but Paul had a different idea. He used this opportunity to tell me about some of the incidents of sexual abuse involving his mother. He began by asking me why his penis was different from that of other boys'. Would I have a look at it? I felt that this was quite a significant conversation, because although obscene language comes easily to Paul, he finds it very difficult to talk about his body and to use words like penis. I am sure this is a characteristic he shares with many other children who have been sexually abused. I also thought he asked me to look at his penis to test out the boundaries of our relationship, to see whether I would respond sexually to him if he gave me a good excuse. I told him I did not think that it was appropriate for me to look at his penis, but that I would ask his dad to do so.

What I failed to consider at the time was that Paul could have been genuinely worried. I had forgotten that his penis would be different from many of his friends' because he had been circumcised. It shows that one can sometimes miss the obvious by always trying to look for the deeper meanings. After being reassured that I was not too tired or too busy to listen to him, Paul asked me why I never "let him have it off" with me, as his natural mother had done. He talked about times he had enjoyed having sex with his mother and how, on occasion, he had instigated it, usually when she was drunk in order to "pay her back" for her abuse of him. Although he spoke in a child's rather than an adult's terminology, it was clear that the sexual involvement with his mother had not been all bad. It was "bad" when it had caused him pain but "good" when he had enjoyed it. Sex to him was a one-way process. He either got pleasure and paid his mother back or was used for her pleasure and got pain. There seemed to be no reciprocal sharing of pleasure.

I repeated the message that in this family we did not behave in the same way as in his natural parents' home. I explained that children often want to do things which are not good for them, usually because they cannot differentiate between enjoyable things which are good for them and enjoyable things which are not. In such cases it is a parent's job to differentiate. I would not, for example, give him — or John for that matter — £5 to spend on sweets because although he would happily munch his way through that amount I knew it would not be good for him. In the same way it would not be good for Paul to have sex with me. Sex between a parent and child was never good, whatever age the child was, six, ten, sixteen or grown up. It was not Paul's fault that sex had happened between himself and his mum. He was not old enough to know that it was one of the things which are not good for children, but his mother had known and she was the one who was responsible.

I added that, although sex was never right for children and never right between parents and their children, this did not mean that sex itself could never be right, as Paul would discover when he became a responsible adult. I asked Paul what he thought I would say if he asked to borrow the car to go to the canoe club. Paul readily agreed that I would say no because he was too young to drive a car. I used this analogy to explain that he was too young for sex. If I agreed to let him borrow the car, it would be my responsibility and not Paul's if he crashed it. If I agreed to have sex with Paul it would not be his fault. It would be mine because I knew he was too young. And this would apply even if Paul instigated or encouraged it.

Paul certainly seemed to understand my message, but he tried to work his way round it by seeing if he could limit my responsibility. He offered to wait until I was drunk or asleep and then have sex with me, very gently. I think he was trying to check out whether there was any situation when sex with me would be all right and when I would say I was not responsible. I was emphatic that I would always be responsible and always be in a position to exercise that responsibility. Paul was also asking me in a coded way how, if I did not let him have sex with me, he could show me that he cared and know that I cared about him. Given his experience, he probably thought that if sex was not all right, then it was not all right to show you care. I told Paul that of course it was all right to show me how much he cared, but not through sex however gentle.

Paul then led the conversation round to asking me how many boyfriends I had had. He suggested that was only fair, because he had told me a great deal about himself. Initially I was tempted, feeling that if I did not share my past with him then he might be less keen to share his with me, but I felt uncomfortable and decided that it was not appropriate. Paul was, in an oblique way, trying to introduce a sexual element into his relationship with me. When I told him more than once that I was not prepared to answer his questions, he became angry and told me to get out of the room. But his anger was feigned. As I was going out the door Paul burst into tears and for the first time cried about his past. I cuddled him for some time until he quietened down, then gave him a goodnight kiss and left him to go to sleep.

It had been a very wearing episode but was surely a major break-through. Paul had been able to admit to positive feelings about his sexual experiences with his mother and to realise that in doing so I did not reject him. He was beginning to put his past into perspective, by not shutting away certain aspects of it. The fact that he was able to cry meant that he was beginning to work through some of his pain.

Mary at the adoption agency confirmed the importance of Paul's disclosure. She approved my handling of the situation, particularly my use of concrete examples in trying to help Paul understand why sexual abuse is wrong. She also agreed that I was right not to share my own past with him, if this made me uncomfortable. In such situations we have to go very much on our instincts. Paul's feigned anger and tears may even have demonstrated that he was relieved not to be burdened by knowledge of my sexual experiences.

Mary's major concern was that Neil seemed to have been excluded. She felt quite strongly that Neil should see himself — and be seen by Paul — as having a significant role in helping Paul and me, whereas Paul needed to recognise that he did not have me to himself. It was important to maintain the relationship which Neil and I had exclusive of Paul and to teach him that one relationship does not detract from the other. I accepted a great deal of what Mary said but it was not easy to work out ways of including Neil, since he was often not at home when Paul discussed his past and since Paul never talked about his feelings with Neil. Furthermore, the opportunities Neil and I had of nurturing our own relationship were limited by the fact that we had very little time on our own.

For two to three weeks there was a marked improvement in some aspects of Paul's behaviour. There were three whole days with no tantrums. Once he managed to go to the canoe club on his own, a major sign of growing independence, and, completely of his own volition, he asked if he could join an athletics club. Although Paul still threatened to run away, these were token threats. I think he was beginning to realise that he really did not want to leave. And, very important, for the first time since Paul came to live with us, Neil and I managed to get a night out on our own. My mum babysat and said Paul behaved well. At last there was a chance to follow Mary's advice.

Paul's need to regress to infancy began to diminish, although I vividly remember one evening when he behaved exactly like the two-year-old grandson of a friend of mine. For once his regression was not disruptive but quite natural, as though the two-year-old had shown him what to do. That Paul should have no idea how toddlers normally behave made me realise how much he had missed as a toddler himself. Several times he asked me to push him round the house in a pram while he sucked a carrot, but such regressions as far back as babyhood were becoming increasingly rare.

Alas, Paul's sexual behaviour showed no improvement and became even more of a problem. I sometimes had great difficulty in extricating myself from his grasp. I had to tell him that I would only give him a kiss if he would put his arms down at his side and let me hold them. Paul also began to make very obvious sexual moves towards me and on one occasion he lay on the settee and made the motions and sounds of someone having sexual intercourse. It was sickening to see this, especially the strange smile on his face. I told Paul that if he wished to masturbate, he should go to his room.

The other major continuing problem was Paul's relationship to other people. He got on well with my mother, but when my niece, Barbara, came to stay with her grandmother there were problems. He resented any attention my mother paid to Barbara, admittedly a very demanding child herself. In the same way, when I had Barbara and Paul together Paul would react by having tantrums. Barbara was horrified and could not understand why I cared about Paul when he treated me so badly.

Another target of Paul's jealousy was Susan. After one of her visits, Paul spent some time digging a knife into a cardboard box and ripping it to shreds. He said he hated Susan and would like to do this to her. Eventually he acknowledged that he did not really want to hurt Susan but he resented not being included in our conversations. He saw her as one of the few people who took attention away from him. He may also have felt vulnerable and wondered to what extent I shared information about him with others, and I think he was resentful that his own social worker, David, had not been visiting and therefore he had no one for himself. Susan was quite taken aback when I told her about Paul's behaviour. We decided she should ask David to spend more time with Paul, while Susan would include Paul in her next interview with us.

It so happened that Susan's next visit was to discuss the Adoption Petition and so was a good excuse to involve Paul. She explained the procedure to Paul who loved being the centre of attention and responded positively. His sense of humour came to the fore and he amused us all by pretending that Neil and I had thrown him out of the boat when we were on holiday. It was a warm, relaxed evening.

By the end of July Paul had reverted to regular tantrums. This came to a head one weekend when Neil was working. As soon as Paul got up that Saturday it was obvious that he was unsettled. Almost immediately he began to behave badly. When I rebuked him he completely lost his temper, tried to kick me, smashed an ornament, demanded his pocket money and swore at me. Eventually he admitted that he was scared, that he wanted to stay with us but knew it was just a matter of time before we sent him back to the children's home. My reassurances had little effect in calming Paul and his tantrum continued on and off all day. I felt Paul's behaviour was partly due to our recent discussion about the Adoption Petition. He must have had mixed feelings, on the one hand pleased that we were demonstrating our commitment to him, but on the other worried about the finality of adoption.

The following day was the adoption agency's summer picnic, which was being held at a park near where Paul had previously lived. I had invited my mother and Barbara to come with us. Both were looking forward to the day out, but in fact it proved to be disastrous. Paul was deeply resentful of Barbara attending the picnic and spent several hours beforehand telling me how he would like to punch and kick her. As soon as we arrived at the park, Paul again demanded his pocket money and when I told him he could not have it until after the picnic and only then if he had behaved well, his mood turned into a tantrum. He disrupted my attempts to join in the games with Barbara by swearing at me and hitting me. Eventually I had no option but to restrain Paul. I caught him and sat on him, telling him that there he would remain for thirty minutes. During that time, he tried to bite me, spit on me and kick me. He continued to use foul language. I tried to remain calm. Just before letting him go I told him that now I expected him to behave. In fact, I expected him to become completely outrageous, but to my surprise the opposite happened. Paul quickly wanted cuddles and reassurance from me.

The other people at the picnic were marvellous. A great many had had experience of dealing with children with behaviour problems and all were very sympathetic to me. One man played with

Paul for a time in order to give me a rest. The next time I went to an agency support group the members said how well I had dealt with Paul. This was a great boost to my confidence. Susan also congratulated me. She was surprised at how he settled as soon as I let him go and thought that his tantrum had been a manipulative exercise designed to test how I would cope in front of a group of people.

Paul's behaviour remained reasonable until the end of the picnic when he had another tantrum and told me that he was definitely running away to the children's home. He then disappeared. I returned to the car and waited for about ten minutes. Just as I was about to go to the children's home, Paul returned. On the way home, he continued to be difficult and swore at my mother who became very upset and started crying.

The whole day was a nightmare. I felt really angry with Paul for upsetting my mum and Barbara and disrupting the picnic. I felt angry that he could treat me so badly. I felt frustrated at the regression after a few weeks of reasonable behaviour. At the same time, I could understand why Paul was behaving in this way. The finality of the Adoption Petition, Barbara's presence, reminding him that she was more a member of our family than he was, and the fact that the picnic was near where he had lived with his natural parents all contributed to his insecurity. The one positive factor was that this was the best opportunity Paul had had to run away to the children's home, since it was only about half a mile away, and he did not take it. This was clear proof to me that Paul did not want to leave us. Yet, no amount of understanding solved the problem of Paul's temper tantrums and I just did not know how long I could continue to cope with the unrelenting pressure of his behaviour.

Susan agreed that these tantrums could not continue, and after considerable discussion we came up with three possible solutions. One was for Neil to take Paul to work with him. This had certainly proved effective when Paul had been behaving badly at school. It was also a way of involving Neil. Another idea was for Susan and David to confront Paul jointly about his behaviour. Neil was concerned this might make Paul feel that he was back in the children's home where his behaviour used to be discussed by the group of staff. However, we decided that desperate measures were needed. The third tactic was more long-term. Susan suggested that we should find time every week to sit down as a family to discuss Paul's behaviour. It had to be made clear to Paul that Neil and I were working together. This was difficult to convey on a day to day basis because Neil was seldom at home when Paul was misbehaving and Paul was nearly always in bed when Neil returned from work, but if we had set times each week Paul would know that he would have to discuss his behaviour with Neil as well as me. Neil hoped he would not be cast in the role of the bad guy but Susan felt that this could be offset by emphasising both the positive and negative aspects of Paul's behaviour.

Our first tactic was a qualified success. We explained to Paul that if he could behave in a reasonable manner when Neil was present, there was no reason why he could not do so when Neil was not there. If he could not, then we would have to ensure that he spent as little time as possible alone with me and so when Neil was on late shifts he would take Paul to work with him. We emphasised that we were not doing this because I could not control him, or because I was rejecting him, but because he must learn that his behaviour towards me would not be tolerated. For some time there was an improvement in Paul's behaviour.

The second tactic was not as effective. David and Susan visited us and tried to talk to Paul as sensitively as possible, but as soon as they confronted him about the unacceptability of his tantrums, Paul left the room and, although he eventually returned, I am not certain to what extent he registered their disapproval. Perhaps Neil was right — four adults confronting one child was too top heavy. Susan and David's joint intervention may also have aroused Paul's fears that we were not coping and that he might have to leave.

As for the third tactic — family discussion — we decided to leave this in abeyance for the time being, as the first tactic seemed to be working well. The tantrums did not cease but because their violence diminished — on one occasion Paul wielded a wooden spoon rather than a knife! — I found I did not always have to restrain him to stop the tantrum. Ignoring him was sometimes just as effective.

We were able to report these improvements to Susan who came to see us just before our second summer holiday. She came to go over the Adoption Petition with us once again. She wanted to be absolutely certain that we were aware that adopting Paul meant making a legal and financial commitment to him as if he were our natural child. If, say, for any reason, Paul could not remain with us, we would still be responsible for maintaining him and he would still have rights of inheritance. Neil and I had of course discussed the nature of the commitment which we would be making to Paul, and we both fully accepted it. After all, we had known what Paul was like before he came to live with us and we had taken him on that basis. We had no compunction in agreeing that the Adoption Petition should be lodged in court. Susan said this would be done by the time we returned from holiday.

Nothing, as we made our way to the airport for the start of our holiday in Rhodes, prepared us for the disaster which it turned out to be. We were all excited, and Neil and I hoped that this holiday, unlike the last, would give us the opportunity to be together as a family. At Glasgow airport and during the flight Paul — a child who had never been out of Scotland let alone flying off in a plane to foreign parts — kept us amused by trying hard to look like a seasoned traveller. When we arrived in Rhodes all went smoothly. Our apartment was in a typical Greek holiday resort, full of cafés and souvenir shops, not much in the way of traditional Greek culture, but everyone seemed friendly and there was a sandy beach near by.

The first cloud on the horizon occurred later that night. We had had dinner and had returned to our room fairly late with the intention of putting Paul to bed and having some time to ourselves. Paul, however, had other ideas. He was deeply resentful of being excluded and the moment we sat outside on the balcony he got up from his bed and started making a nuisance of himself. He grabbed my bottle of wine, threatened to pour the contents down the sink, and when this produced no response he locked us outside. I thought we should just continue to ignore Paul, that eventually he would get bored, but Neil became furious and shouted at him to open the door. When Paul did not immediately do this, Neil banged on the glass. The glass shattered, leaving jagged edges in the frame, and Neil stepped through and badly cut his leg. There was blood and glass everywhere and I had to rush downstairs for help. Fortunately the apartment owner was extremely helpful and took us to the hospital where Neil was given a number of stitches.

This incident blighted the entire holiday. Neil was in some pain and had difficulty walking. He was angry with Paul and Paul was resentful of Neil. I think Paul felt that he was being blamed for something which was not his fault and I tended to agree. Neil had over-reacted to Paul's behaviour and Paul could not be held responsible for Neil breaking a glass door and then cutting himself. I blamed Neil for the accident. I also resented the fact that Neil's injury left me with the entire burden of organising our activities and looking after Paul for several days.

The atmosphere of this anger and resentment must have exacerbated Paul's behaviour which was, to say the least, horrendous. With the exception of two days, tantrums dominated our holiday. Increasingly, these tantrums became directed at Neil, who reacted by becoming more and more angry with Paul, who would retaliate by throwing stones at Neil. I was particularly nervous when this happened one day as we were walking down a street lined with shops with plate glass windows.

In one way, Paul's behaviour could be seen as progress. He was now beginning to test Neil's commitment to him and we had always known he would have to do this before he could really settle with us. I felt our approach should be to reassure Paul that Neil was committed to him, no matter how difficult and aggressive he was. Neil agreed but also felt Paul must be made aware how unacceptable his behaviour was by being punished for it. I suppose the basic difference between us was that I focused on Paul's problems and the reasons for his tantrums, while Neil was trying to treat him as a normal boy who was behaving badly. On reflection all that mattered was that Paul got both the messages, that Neil was committed to him *and* that his behaviour was unacceptable, but Neil and I argued constantly. I accused him of being too punitive towards Paul, while he accused me of being too soft. We were certainly not working together and it is not surprising that Paul was able to use his tantrums to good effect to widen the gulf between Neil and me.

On several occasions Neil chose to opt out of a crisis and walked off leaving me with Paul. I felt this was most unfair of Neil and eventually I became so angry that I issued both Paul and Neil with an ultimatum. Unless they both made an effort to behave better, then I would walk off for a few days of peace and quiet on my own. This had a marvellous effect. For the first time during the holiday Paul and Neil were united — against me perhaps. They both took my remarks seriously and made an effort to improve. Paul actually managed the next day without a major tantrum.

While Paul was becoming increasingly aggressive towards Neil, he was becoming increasingly possessive of me. If I sat at a bus stop, he would immediately sit on my knee and try to kiss me, if I stood up he would cling to me. He tried to interrupt virtually every conversation I had with Neil and felt threatened if I tried to spend any time alone with Neil. Every night, after dinner, Paul would go on and on asking me if I would be sitting out on the balcony with his dad until I felt like screaming. By the end of the holiday his jealousy of Neil was becoming even more obvious. He often asked me if I would divorce Neil so that he could be my boyfriend. Neil, for his part, became so irritated with Paul continually pawing me that for a whole day he pawed Paul himself! Paul began to understand how overwhelmed I must feel and he tried to be less clinging. It was a wonderful relief.

Another bad sign was that Paul's threats to run away re-emerged. He continually told us that he hated living with us and wanted to return to the children's home. Whenever he stormed off I would follow him, concerned about the danger of him being on his own in a strange town. Once I held onto him during a bus journey to prevent him getting off at every stop. I soon realised that I was only making the situation worse. Paul was adept at using these threats to get a reaction from me when other tactics failed. Neil rightly insisted that I should not follow Paul when he disappeared one day in Rhodes town and reassured me that Paul would make his way to the stop where we caught the bus back to our apartment. This is indeed what happened. Paul was very upset that we had not followed him and did not disappear again during the holiday.

The holiday had a few positive moments. We took part in a village dance, visited a Greek theatre, shopped for souvenirs, Paul caught a lizard, and we enjoyed the excitement of a midnight swim. Even so, I was relieved when the time came to return to Scotland and I think Neil and Paul felt the same.

Although I was often very angry with Paul during the holiday, I could not really blame him for its failure. I was so convinced that a holiday abroad, travelling by air, would be a wonderful new experience for him that I never stopped to consider some of the disadvantages. Paul, like Neil, is very active, and in a country where it is too hot to do much it is not surprising that he got bored. Greece must also have come as a complete culture shock to him. Neither can he have found it any easier than we did to have a tiny apartment with little privacy for any of us, while being so far away from home must have unsettled him and contributed to his difficult behaviour. For the first time in his life Paul was totally dependent on two people with no means of escape. If we had stopped to consider any of these issues, I am sure we would never have gone either on the boat holiday or to Rhodes. It is important for a foster or adoptive parent to choose a holiday which meets the child's needs, not one which the parent fondly imagines the child will enjoy. We certainly learned a lesson from our two disastrous holidays and the next year we planned our holiday carefully round Paul. We remained in Scotland, having an active time, and all three of us enjoyed ourselves much more.

9
UPS AND DOWNS

After our holiday Paul returned to school and Neil and I to work. We got back to our normal routine and for a time Paul's behaviour improved, as did our relations towards each other. Paul seemed more relaxed in school, largely because he was now in a class of only twenty children with one very experienced teacher (the assistant headmistress) who seemed to understand his problems. Once Paul found it easier to cope he was under less pressure to misbehave. He began to relate better to his peers and even talked positively about his teachers. Early reports indicated that he was settling down to do some work and, although he was behind in most subjects, his teacher was confident that he had the ability to catch up. One improvement I noticed almost immediately was his handwriting. When Paul had first come to live with us his writing was so small and light that it was quite illegible and I could not persuade him to write more distinctly. Now his writing became larger and darker and I was able to read and understand it. It was as though Paul was beginning to trust us enough not to feel he had to keep his written thoughts from us.

We were pleased that Paul was beginning to make friends at school. His particular friend, Graham, was in the same class, a cheerful, cheeky child. He was much more mature than Paul and, although I know he got into trouble in school and in the local community, he was certainly better adjusted. It was surprising to me that Paul seemed to get on well with Graham and visited him at his home. The first time I collected Paul, I found the house poorly furnished and rather grubby and Graham's parents, although caring and welcoming, not very bright. I admit I felt uncomfortable there. Perhaps Paul was right, I was a 'snob'. Paul, on the other hand, seemed much more relaxed there than he ever did in our house. This made me realise just how much of a cultural change Paul had had to accept when he came to live with us and how little I had taken this into consideration when analysing his behaviour. He must have felt just as uncomfortable in our home as I had felt in Graham's, but whereas I could get up and leave, Paul had no such escape. I had always thought that, for Paul, joining our family meant us offering him new opportunities. I failed to realise how much he had had to give up. The fact that, six months after he had come to live with us, Paul still seemed more comfortable in Graham's home than ours is testimony to just how difficult it must have been for him.

Another positive development came when Paul asked if he could join the local scout troop. This was an important sign that he felt sufficiently secure in his relationship with us to develop some independence from us. He was beginning to move beyond the exclusive stage of development. Was he also beginning to accept that Neil and I could be allowed some time on our own? After all, Paul knew that I could not join the scouts and that Neil and I would have one night (two hours to be precise!) without him and the opportunity of going out together. We certainly took advantage of these times and made an agreement to spend no more than the first half hour talking about Paul! However, it was several months before Paul could relax at the scouts' evenings. Although he certainly talked enthusiastically about the various activities on offer, his enjoyment and ability to participate were very much tempered by his concern about what Neil and I were doing. When he got home he would ask what we had done and where we had been, anxious lest he should be left out.

Paul's tantrums were becoming more manageable. So was his sexual behaviour. Previously, when Paul used goodnight kisses as an opportunity to behave inappropriately towards me, I had to control him physically, by holding his arms to his side or persuading him to put them under the covers. I now tried to control him verbally, reminding him every night what was and what was not an acceptable kiss. I then gave him the opportunity to kiss me appropriately. If he did not think he could manage this, it was fine to tell me so and then I would hold him. Paul's response to this varied. Sometimes he gave me an acceptable kiss and cuddle, sometimes he told me it was too difficult and I held him, sometimes he said he would behave but failed to do so. Increasingly, though, when Paul did not think he could control himself, he would admit it rather than pretend.

I thought it would be useful to introduce Paul to some of the liter-

ature on sexual behaviour. The book I used,[2] had been given me by
Paul's social worker, but I had not found an opportunity to introduce it to Paul that did not seem contrived. As it happened, Paul
came across the book by chance. I said he could read it if he
wished. As he began to flick through the pages, he became very
embarrassed and asked if he could take it to his bedroom. Of
course I agreed, and later when he told me that he had found it
quite amusing, I suggested that we might read it together and perhaps talk about its content. After considerable hesitation Paul not
only agreed to this but also that Neil should join in the discussion.
The book is about good, bad and secret touching and uses explicit
words such as penis and vagina to describe various parts of the
human body, but the material is presented in a humorous way, so
we were able to discuss the different types of touching in a relaxed
atmosphere. Even though Paul never related the material to his
own experiences, I felt it was a very positive occasion. Bringing the
subject of sexual behaviour into an open forum and involving Neil
would, I hoped, give Paul the clear message that it was not wrong to
talk about sexuality and in particular about the sexual abuse which
he had experienced. Later events certainly justified my hopes. It is
not always at the time that parents reap the benefit of working with
their children.

That said, there was to be a revealing negative outcome of our
discussion. Some time later Paul referred me to a statement in the
touching book which implies that one of the reasons why the sexual
abuse of children by adults is wrong is that it could spoil sexual
experiences for a child when he or she grows up. Paul had said
before that his "parents had fucked away his childhood". He now
asked if, in view of the statement in the book, his parents had not
only ruined his childhood but also his adulthood. In short, had his
parents "fucked away his adulthood"?

I was completely unprepared for this question. I had to answer in
such a way as not to contradict what I had previously said about sex
between adults and children being wrong. I was totally taken aback
by the depth in which Paul had considered the issues in the book
and upset at the pain which Paul must have suffered in silence
before he felt able to talk to me.

I did what I suppose must people would do in this situation. I
bought time and surprised myself when inspiration came. I

[2] Jan Hindman. *A Very Touching Book*. Oregon: McClure–Hindman Associates, 1985.

acknowledged that Paul's experiences gave him knowledge of sex which other children lacked. Although this might make adult sexual experience different for him and was one of the reasons why it was wrong for an adult sexually to abuse a child, this did not mean that adult sexual experiences would be less special for him or blighted by his past. I told him that sex between two adults was not and never could be the same as sex between an adult and a child. With the help of the touching book I talked to Paul about the sexual organs of the body, about orgasms and the release of sperm, and explained how children's bodies mature and change during adolescence. Only then can they enjoy sex in a complete, adult way, a way he could not have experienced with his mother. Paul then asked me to describe in detail what sexual intercourse between two adults was like. Only his acceptance and lack of embarrassment made it possible for me to do so in a relaxed manner. (Adults have a lot to learn from children.) By the end of the discussion Paul seemed satisfied that his parents had not "fucked away" his adulthood. Despite my lack of preparation and hesitancy, my answers served the purpose. Children do not look for perfect expert explanations. What matters is what makes sense to the child.

I then introduced the term 'sexual abuse'. I had never previously talked to Paul in a general way about personal experiences, as I had not wanted to add to his trauma, but the above discussion highlighted how capable he was of accepting factual explanations. I felt that what Paul now needed more than anything was to see his experience as something beyond which he could move, to become aware that what he had suffered was not unique, so I told him that there were many children who had had similar experiences to his and that what had happened to him and those other children was called 'sexual abuse'. These children had been able to work through their experience and come to terms with it and I hoped that this would give Paul confidence to do the same. Although sexual abuse had made them feel very mixed up and angry, many were now happily married with children of their own. Without minimising the problems and anguish sexual abuse creates for its victims, I tried to bring home to Paul that it does not have to ruin a child's life.

At the end of the conversation I reminded him, as I always did, that if he wanted to ask me anything else I would be there. I kissed him goodnight (very important on these occasions) and let him go to sleep.

Three meetings were held during the autumn to assess Paul's progress with us. The first was a review involving ourselves and staff from the adoption agency and the social work department. We reported the problems we had had with Paul during our holidays as well as the recent improvement, and a comparison with the previous review made us very much aware of the progress Paul had achieved since he came to stay with us. This was particularly heartening for it is often difficult to look beyond the immediate situation and put it in perspective. However, I did take exception to a comment that we must be pleased to be able to say something positive about Paul. There had never been a time when I had not been able to say something positive about him! It is vitally important for adoptive parents to be able to do this. We choose our particular child for his or her positive qualities.

Perhaps the best news we heard was that the Adoption Petition had been submitted. Paul, unusually for him, agreed to attend the latter part of the review. His social worker told him the positive aspects of our previous discussion and how pleased he was that Paul was beginning to settle with us. The area manager spelled out the implications of the Adoption Petition for us all. Paul had "made it, he had found his new family", and nothing was going to change that. This gave Paul official confirmation of what we had been telling him for months. He looked pleased and I felt all the waiting and work had been worthwhile, that I had "made it", too.

The second meeting was a discussion between David (Paul's social worker), Susan (our social worker), Jane (Paul's psychologist), and Neil and me. Jane had known Paul since he was seven years old, so we particularly valued her opinion. We knew that she would be able to put the past six months into the context of the three years she had been working with Paul. She was delighted at the progress Paul had made, expressing surprise that he had come so far in such a short time, and pleased both that Paul was beginning to share so much about his past with us and at the way in which we had dealt with his sexuality. At the same time Jane predicted that Paul would test out the relationship between Neil and me much more assertively in the future and would continue to compete with Neil for my affections. Paul might begin to model himself on Neil, to see if Neil's position in the family could be usurped, but in the process he could well grow fonder of Neil. If this ambivalence was sensitively handled, a closer relationship between the two could emerge.

Thirdly, I was given the opportunity to attend a two-day training session for foster parents working with children who have been sexually abused. The first day was extremely informative and helpful, with parents sharing their experiences. On the second day we were shown part of a very powerful video, *The Nightingale Roars*,[3] compiled by a woman who had suffered sexual abuse as a child. I borrowed the video and watched it right through at home. It was a traumatic experience. Emotions which I had submerged during very difficult periods with Paul and had refused to share with Neil, thus cutting myself off from his support, were forced to the fore and I cried for nearly two hours, not simply for Paul but for myself and all that I had gone through in the past six months. It was wonderfully therapeutic. That night for the first time Neil and I talked about what it really felt like to be responsible for a difficult and disturbed child. It seemed as though we were at last relating together as Paul's parents.

After the review, Paul began to accept that he was now part of the family and also, to some extent, the role which Neil and I had in his life. At times he seemed only too glad that I should cope with and tolerate his behaviour. However, any attempts at what might be called normal care — taking an interest in what he was doing, helping with homework, imposing reasonable standards in terms of personal hygiene and bedtimes — were likely to be met with resentment and comments like, "I don't need anyone to help me or tell me what to do" or "I can look after myself, I don't need you". This was understandable because Paul's parents had never offered him any care. However, as he began to accept that he was remaining with us, he also began to accept that he had a right and desire to be cared for. One of the first signs of this occurred when we were walking along a rocky part of the beach and I tripped. Paul's spontaneous reaction was, "Watch you don't hurt yourself, mum. I've spent too long caring for one mum, now it's my turn to be looked after". He explained that when his mother was drunk, he had to fend for himself as well as making sure that she was all right. I reassured Paul that he would not have to care for me and that as a mum I expected to do the caring. Paul seemed pleased.

However, Paul was not always pleased when I exercised my responsibilities as a mother. His recent progress was not main-

---

[3] See also Catherine MacAskill. *Adopting or Fostering a Sexually Abused Child.* London: Batsford, 1991.

tained and he started to behave unreasonably again. I was not too disheartened, because I know that every new phase Paul goes through creates pressure and confusion for him. In this particular phase he wanted to be cared for and yet feared I might take advantage of him and interfere. One minute he was rushing up asking me to knot his school tie. The next minute he was fiercely independent telling me to stop fussing, that he did not need me to do things for him; invariably the result was a tantrum.

An entirely new facet of Paul's behaviour at this time was crying. He would burst into tears at every opportunity if he could not have his own way, or if he tripped and fell. Something as simple as refusing him another biscuit brought on the tears. This was very different from Paul's usual pretended unconcern. We had never known him to get upset about anything. Even when he hurt himself he rushed away out of sight so that we could not see him crying. I was really puzzled and did not know whether this was progress or regression. Susan suggested that in fact Paul's crying was a very positive sign. His hard aggressive behaviour was a means of coping with his suffering and the only way he could progress was to discard his defence mechanism and start to feel again. She thought that Paul's crying over small issues was the beginning of this process and hoped that he would be able to move on to crying about more important things and thereby begin to come to terms with the major traumas in this life. I reminded Susan of the almost matter-of-fact way Paul described incidents of sexual abuse to me and how he rarely became distressed or upset. She thought that he was on the way to moving beyond the telling to the feeling.

A few weeks later Susan was proved right. Paul had had a bad tantrum and went to bed still agitated. I asked him what had happened to make him so angry, as he did not often act as badly now. Paul told me that it was none of my business, a sure sign he had something important to say. Eventually, after I persisted, he started talking about his past, but kept reminding me that he had told me about it before. There was no point in going over it again, it made no difference. This seemed to me to be the crux of the matter and I asked Paul if he thought that telling me what had happened to him would make him forget it. "Yes", he said, "I thought it would, but it hasn't". I felt so sorry for him. As gently as I could I told him that he would always remember what had happened to him, that telling me about it would not and could not make it go away; but these were not the only memories he now had. He had memories about his foster parents, the children's home and his time with us and in due course as new memories, good and bad, increased, the memories about his past would become less painful. They would never go away completely but they would mean less and less to him. I told Paul that talking sometimes helped to speed up healing and asked him if it had made a difference. Paul agreed that it had, that he did not feel quite as bad as before he had told me. And, yes, he was beginning to have some nice memories and to think a little less about the bad things in his past.

When I discussed this episode with Susan, she suggested that from time to time I should talk to Paul about our good memories. I tried to do this in a casual way about fairly minor things, such as the previous time we had been to a particular park or enjoyed a particular game. I hoped this would also remind Paul that he had been with us for some time and make him feel more secure.

Soon after the review Paul's friendship with Graham began to wane. I think Graham got fed up having such a childish friend. Paul was aware of this. In fact he told me that Graham's three-year-old brother acted towards his mother exactly as he acted towards me. "He is just as much of a sop-ball as I am." I do not think Paul was perturbed by this comparison, but it may have helped him to recognise what he was doing. Graham for his part was astounded at the way in which Paul would kiss and cuddle me. I was not entirely surprised at Graham's embarrassment but at the same time I felt he was not a particularly good influence on Paul and was quite relieved when Paul told me that he now had a new friend, John.

Now the tables were reversed. John was a shy, nervous child and I was worried that Paul would adversely influence his new friend. I liked John and enjoyed having him in our house. He and Paul were polar opposites. He became quite upset when Paul lost his temper and started swearing at me and would tell Paul that he should not behave in that way. He was lucky to have such a nice mum who gave him so much of her time and attention. Maybe this helped Paul to realise how much he was being offered by us.

Paul's friendship with John led to one of the most embarrassing moments in my life (and subsequently to a revealing discussion with Paul). One evening when John was visiting us Paul brought up the subject of AIDS. It had been receiving a great deal of media attention and Paul is always interested in sexual matters. Both boys started asking me what AIDS was and how it was caught, and as I was trying my best to answer their questions, Paul suddenly turned round to John and said, "My mum raped me," and then to me, "Didn't she mum?". There was a stunned silence. I could not refute Paul's claim because it was absolutely true. Yet agreement might have led to entirely inappropriate explanations and discussions. I wanted to say that *I* was not the mum who had "raped" Paul, that *I* was not to blame, in case there was any chance John might think me guilty of sexual abuse. In fact there was nothing I could say and poor John looked completely mystified. I responded simply by jumping up and changing the subject.

Later, after we had taken John home, I spoke to Paul about his remark. I felt a certain ambivalence about doing this. I did not want to make Paul feel guilty and ashamed about his past, but I wanted to protect him from discussing his past with people who would not understand and might even shun him. It was an extremely difficult discussion. I knew that one of the problems of sexual abuse was that children were often told to keep it a secret and threatened with dire consequences if they did not. I was not certain whether this had happened to Paul, but I did know that it had been difficult for him to talk and I had told him then that I was glad that he had shared his secret with me. I could not now tell him that his experiences were something which should be kept secret. The way I got round this was to emphasise how brave and right he had been to share his past with me but to explain that, although I was able to understand what he was saying, some people, like John and probably most of his other friends, were not. I suggested it might be better to reserve his disclosures for those people who understood about sexual abuse.

I must have been at least partially successful in not giving Paul the impression that he had anything to be ashamed of, because he used the opportunity to talk more about the sexual abuse he had suffered. Previously Paul had talked in general terms about what had happened to him. On this occasion he went into more detail about the circumstances. Abuse usually took place when his mother was drunk and often after arguments with his father. Paul would be sent upstairs and she would follow and abuse him. Paul insisted that it was some time before his dad knew — and participated in — what was happening. He was adamant that his dad never actually abused him. Paul therefore feels that his dad was blameless in this respect and is not able (or perhaps prepared) to see that by condoning the abuse he was almost as guilty as his wife. If anything I felt angrier with him than with Paul's mother. Perhaps because Paul loathes his mother, a justifiable emotion, whereas he liked his father. A few weeks later I asked Paul if he ever felt anger towards his dad or blamed him at all for what had happened. Paul's response was "Well perhaps - I don't think so". Maybe it was something he could not yet cope with or perhaps his dad was more involved in the abuse than Paul had revealed. It was not the time to delve any deeper.

The major problem area during the three months following the review was undoubtedly school. At the review Paul had been praised for settling down at school and beginning to work to his potential. Almost immediately afterwards his behaviour deteriorated dramatically, as though he had decided to prove to everyone that he was not a well-behaved child and that the positive comments at the review had seriously questioned his sense of identity.

For a time Paul continued to cope well in class, but during unstructured times he was disruptive in the extreme. He would run round the school playground, refusing to do as he was told and becoming increasingly aggressive to other children, generally those younger and more vulnerable than himself. Often when he lost his temper he would subject both peers and adults to a barrage of abusive language. As we had very regular contact with the school we were aware of these problems and tried every way we could to encourage Paul to develop a more positive approach to school. We bought him books to try and motivate an interest in learning and we helped him with his homework, we praised him when he had a good day at school, we punished him by withholding treats, and we constantly reinforced the message that he could behave if he wanted. Nothing worked and about a month after the review we received yet another in a long line of telephone calls from the school to say that Paul had lashed out at a child and that something must be done, if nothing else to demonstrate to other children that such behaviour was unacceptable. The school at this point was very sympathetic to Paul. There was a new head teacher, and although she had a more traditional approach to discipline than her predecessor she seemed to want to help Paul. She invited us to go to the school the following morning to discuss the problem. We agreed that the standard three-day suspension would be counter-productive, giving Paul just what he wanted and in fact rewarding him for his bad behaviour. Instead Neil would take Paul to his school for three days. This would show him that removal from school was not an easy option. When we told Paul, he was quite upset, which we interpreted as a positive sign. Going to his dad's work was very different from the suspension he had hoped for.

When Paul returned to school we agreed, first, that he should be kept in during breaks, except for lunchtimes when he would go to my mother, and, second, that we would telephone the school on a daily basis not just twice a week, so we could monitor Paul's behaviour consistently. This seemed to work for a few days, until Paul deliberately emptied the contents of a rubbish bin all over the playground. When the school janitor asked Paul to pick up the rubbish, Paul refused and subjected the poor man to a mouthful of abuse in front of other children. The headmistress made it clear that, while she appreciated how very disturbed Paul was, the school could not continue to tolerate such behaviour. Paul's own teacher was more positive. She felt that they were making progress with Paul and was at pains to stress how well he performed in class when he settled down to work. She was more interested in the reasons for Paul's behaviour than the school's inability to cope with it, and Neil and I did our best to explain Paul's difficulties with reference to his past and his parents. Eventually it was agreed not to suspend Paul on that occasion; but even while we were still talking he hit a girl and gave her a black eye. I was in despair. The headmistress was incensed but, unbelievably, still did not suspend Paul. She insisted he apologised to the girl and, equally unbelievably, he did so.

It was the shortest reprieve. After another, particularly bad, outbreak, the school felt it had no option but to suspend Paul for three days. On this occasion we kept Paul at home. Neil took time off and spent the day doing school work with him. We hoped this would prove to Paul that he could not get out of working simply by being suspended, but if anything it encouraged him to further bad behaviour. Paul enjoyed the one-to-one attention which Neil gave him and interpreted it as a reward not a punishment. During the next suspension when Neil again took time off, he insisted instead that Paul spent the normal school hours alone in his room. He gave him work to do but otherwise largely ignored him. That weekend we continued this tactic of keeping Paul at a distance but with distressingly negative results. Paul became increasingly resentful and indifferent. We could "do anything we liked", punish him in any way we wanted, he did not care. It did not bother him to be sent to his room. "You live in your world and I'll live in mine."

Both Neil and I were at the end of our tether. Paul seemed able to switch off completely and would spend hours in his room, simply lying in his bed, doing nothing. He would make little attempt to read, to play with anything, to communicate with us. I had never known Paul to be distant and uncaring. Ignoring him had made him retreat into his own world; now trying to communicate with him failed to elicit any meaningful conversation. He showed a total lack of concern for us and we had no means of getting through to him the point that behaviour in school, or anywhere else for that matter, was important. In many ways this was more difficult to cope with than the tantrums.

Neil in particular was rightly concerned about how long the school situation could be sustained. Hardly had Paul returned to school but he was suspended again. Again Neil took time off work to look after him, but what tactic to employ? We both felt that Paul's hard uncaring attitude was a very regressive step, that he was totally removing himself from any relationship with us and that the only way to get through to him was to break down this barrier of indifference. However, whereas I argued that sending Paul to his room for prolonged periods only fostered his feeling of total alienation and that we should instead constantly confront him about the undesirability of his behaviour, Neil thought that this would merely give Paul the attention he wanted. By insisting that he remain in his room, apart from mealtimes, during the three-day suspension, Neil hoped that Paul would soon tire of living in his own world and want to relate to us and then we could lay down rules for improved behaviour at school. Neil won the argument, largely because it was he who took time off work to care for Paul. Paul therefore spent virtually three whole days in his room and although occasionally he looked bored and tried to entice the dog into his room, his isolation did not have the desired effect and at the end of it he was still telling us that he wanted to live in his own world.

It was a nightmare period in our lives. We did not know where to turn next. Naturally, we discussed the problem with Susan and, due to the seriousness of the situation, with Jane. Jane felt Paul was testing out areas where Neil and I were most vulnerable. He knew that almost any behaviour he produced in the house was within our control. Our Achilles heel was in the school situation, as this would put pressure on either Neil or me to take time off work. Jane felt that it was imperative that Paul did not disrupt our work. We must make it clear to him that we were neither going to give him up, nor our jobs. She hoped Paul would settle down sufficiently to be able to remain in mainstream education, but suggested that we should also look at alternatives in case his behaviour did not improve. She also suggested that, rather than punish Paul for bad behaviour, we should reward him for good behaviour, perhaps by giving him a treat at the weekend if he had behaved well in school. Punishment only reinforced his own feelings that he was bad and could therefore be counterproductive.

In theory this was fine. We accepted all that Jane said and our attempt to re-emphasise to Paul that he was with us on a permanent basis was greatly helped by the good news that the adoption had been granted. At an interview shortly before, Paul had clearly stated that he would like to be adopted. This was his first verbal admission that he wanted us to be his parents and his first acceptance of his commitment to us. We were very encouraged.

In many ways the actual event was rather an anti-climax. We first heard about it on the telephone from Susan. Considering what an important event the adoption was in our lives, we felt that it deserved more than a telephone call and asked Susan to write to Paul. We agreed not to say anything to him about the adoption until he got the letter. We thought that seeing it in writing would make it more real to Paul and that *he* might like to tell *us* about it. Susan agreed and, true to her word, Paul received a letter the following day. Paul's reaction was odd. He said nothing until I asked him what was in the letter. Obviously I expressed delight at the news and told Paul how pleased I was that he was now officially our son. I suggested we should celebrate by going out for a meal, something Paul normally loves. I thought he would leap at the opportunity, but he was reluctant. Neil was on a late shift and would not be home before 11.00 p.m. Paul said that as he had been adopted by his dad as well as by me, it was not fair for us to go out for a meal without Neil. He suggested that we waited until the weekend to celebrate as a threesome. This was progress indeed. Paul was, at last, not only accepting me as his mother but also demonstrating that he wanted a relationship with Neil and was coming to terms with Neil's role in the family.

Of course I agreed to postpone the meal. However, I did encourage Paul to talk about the granting of the adoption. What did it mean to him? Did it make him feel any more committed to us? Paul said the adoption did not make him feel any different towards us, but it did show him that we wanted him and could not send him back. As this was exactly what the adoption did mean, I was pleased that Paul thought about it in this way. It was exactly the message which Jane had emphasised Paul needed to hear.

Following on from our discussion with Jane, I tried to work on Paul's conception of himself. He often told me that he was 'bad' and that this was why he behaved badly. I would tell him that he was not 'bad' and that, although he sometimes behaved unacceptably, he was perfectly capable of behaving well. When he did behave well and I commented on this, he went out of his way to deny my comments and to behave outrageously. It was as though behaving well, being 'good', questioned his conception of himself. I felt that I had to challenge this conception, but in a way which did not destroy his self-identity without replacing it with a more pleasing identity. My policy of praising his achievements and using terms such as 'unacceptable' rather than 'bad' in relation to his behaviour had obviously not been particularly successful. So I tried another tactic. I picked up a piece of paper and headed one side 'bad things which I do' and the other side 'good things which I do'. On the first side I wrote down some of the very obvious 'bad things' — temper tantrums, swearing, aggression. On the other side I wrote down some of the positive aspects — nice smile, good personality, tells good jokes, handsome. I then handed him the paper and pointed out that the good side was far fuller than the bad side and that I would only accept that he was bad if he could fill up the bad side to balance the good. Paul reacted with comments like "do you really think I'm handsome?", "do you really think I have a good personality?". When I said I did, he visibly relaxed and made no attempt to complete the bad side despite my challenge. I was convinced I had made an impact, and several weeks later I found the paper under his pillow to prove it.

However, other tactics did not work so well. The next time Paul was suspended from school, neither Neil nor I took time off work but insisted that he went to his nan. We hoped to make Paul see that he could not use suspension as a mechanism to force us to give up our jobs, but I now realise that, by this time, nothing would have helped Paul to behave better in school. Paul had got himself into a position where the expectation was that he would misbehave. He was on a downward spiral and did not have the means to climb off.

Jane had suggested we reward Paul more for good behaviour, but how do you reward a child whose behaviour never seems to be reasonable and how do you cope with your anger and frustration and your desire to punish a child who constantly throws everything you try to do for him back in your face? If the problems had only been school-based the situation might have been more manageable, but the swearing and shouting continued as well as the sexual and regressive behaviour. Paul challenged everything we asked him to do and any attempt to speak to him about his behaviour was met with hostility. To make matters worse, Neil and I had frequent disputes over the best way to handle him. I thought Neil was too punitive. Neil thought I was too lenient. We also had different standards. I felt that if Paul had had a good day at school, he had to let off steam and some sort of tantrum was to be expected later on. Neil thought tantrums were unacceptable at any time. I argued it was unreasonable to expect so much so soon and that the most important thing at this stage was to stabilise the school situation. Jane had made it clear that Neil and I should be consistent in our approach to Paul and should back each other up. This was well nigh impossible and, although we never disagreed openly, Paul must have been aware of the different standards expected of him.

The situation came to a head early in December. It was a Friday and Neil had collected Paul from school at the request of the headmistress after Paul had yet again hit out at a child. Neil sent Paul to his room with the instruction that he should remain there until told to come out.

I arrived home unaware of what had happened and looking forward to going out with Neil as it was Paul's evening for scouts. I found Neil agitated and Paul was angry and resentful. Neil wanted Paul to stay in his room for the rest of the night, but when I pointed out that scout evening was the only time in the week when Paul seemed able to relate to peers in an acceptable manner and also that it would be our only opportunity for a break during a weekend which was likely to be difficult, Neil eventually came round to my way of thinking. I told Paul how angry and disappointed we were with him but that Neil and I were prepared to postpone any discussion about school until Sunday night so that it did not ruin the weekend. I suggested that he changed into his scout uniform and joined us for dinner. I thought that Paul would jump at this opportunity to retrieve the situation but instead he shouted and swore that he did not mind staying in his room, that he did not want any dinner, and he was not going to the scouts.

I tried three times to reason with Paul but made no progress. (Perhaps the thought of leaving Neil and me together was too much for him to cope with. He may have been afraid that sending him to the scouts was an indirect way of rejecting him.) Instead of changing into his scout uniform, he put on his skiing salopettes over his other clothes. I was so angry. I had given Paul every opportunity to reach a compromise. I also saw my chance of getting out for a short time rapidly receding. I told Paul not to be so silly and to take off his salopettes.

A struggle ensued, with the two of us ending up on the floor. At this stage Neil intervened, grabbed Paul and pulled him along by his shirt collar which tightened round Paul's neck and made red marks. Paul became extremely upset and screamed at Neil, "You're choking me". Neil ignored this, got Paul into a chair and started shouting at him. Paul cried hysterically and kept repeating, "You were trying to choke me". At this, my anger with Paul dissolved and transferred to Neil. I shouted at him to shut up. Could he not see that he had hurt Paul and was upsetting him further by his shouting? I got between the two and, bending over to comfort Paul, told him that I was sorry his dad had acted in this way. At the same time I told Neil that I would never allow a child of mine to be hurt and that if such a situation ever occurred again he would be asked to leave the house. Neil completely lost his temper and threatened to hit Paul who was obviously now really scared. He rushed into another room and hid under a desk.

My loyalties were entirely with Paul. I followed him and tried to calm him. I told him that I was sure his dad had not meant to hurt and threaten him and that he could spend the remainder of the evening with me. Paul, although still tearful and upset, calmed down. He helped me make dinner and even managed to eat most of it. Neil refused dinner but later on clearly regretted what had happened and apologised to Paul for losing his temper. He reassured him he would never threaten him with violence again. No matter how outrageously a child behaves, he has a right to expect not to be hurt. Adults were responsible for their own behaviour and he was sorry if he had frightened Paul. All three of us ended up in tears. Paul admitted that his behaviour had contributed to the eruption, but he was still tense and a little afraid of Neil.

The following day I began to consider the implications of what had happened. We would have to report the incident to Susan and I wondered how she would view it. Would she think our house was a safe place for Paul? What would happen if she decided that it was not? There was also the fear of losing face. Here we were, supposedly caring and coping parents, reporting a situation which had got totally out of control. As I blamed Neil for putting me in this situation it was impossible for us to have a rational discussion. Neil accepted the blame and was angry with himself. Yet I was not prepared to acknowledge how upset he was at acting in a way which, by his own standards, was inappropriate. Before Paul had been placed with us, Neil and I had decided that he should never be smacked or threatened with physical chastisement. I was deeply upset that this agreement had been breached. I told Neil I had no sympathy for him. It was therefore for him to telephone Susan to take responsibility for what had happened and then deal with the consequences.

In the end my worst fears were groundless. Susan agreed that Neil had gone beyond acceptable limits but as he had not intended to hurt Paul she was confident that Paul was not at risk in our house. Because of the inordinate difficulties we had in parenting Paul, she was more interested in looking at ways of avoiding a similar situation from recurring. She identified the point where Neil intervened in the struggle between Paul and me as the catalyst. Neil's interpretation was that he was acting in support of me. I felt he was doing the opposite, that he had taken over and was undermining me. Eventually, we decided on two basic rules which I would recommend all foster and adoptive parents should attempt to abide by when dealing with children who have been badly abused. First, physical punishment would not be used at all. Even threats of physical punishment were inappropriate. In view of Paul's history of ill-treatment, the message needed to be strongly reinforced that adults were safe people who would not hurt him. Second, if I was in a situation with Paul which looked like getting out of control, Neil should check with me what I would find most helpful before intervening, In the same way I should check with Neil before I intervened. It was important that Neil and I were seen to be working together to manage Paul's behaviour, rather than allow Paul to 'divide and rule'.

Susan felt, however, that by far the most damaging aspect of the entire situation was my statement to Paul that his dad would be told in no uncertain terms to leave if he ever hurt Paul again. I did what we had always maintained would militate against a successful placement. Paul desperately needed two parents, and here I was endorsing a relationship between Paul and me which excluded Neil. I had felt I was acting correctly to protect Paul from potential harm and had not until now thought of the wider implications. With Susan acting as referee, Neil and I began to see the other's point of view.

By the end of the session, although I was still adamant that no child of mine should ever be hurt, I could understand why Neil had reacted as he did, while Neil, appreciating my abhorrence of violence towards children, realised he must work on controlling his temper. When Paul arrived home we were much more united. Susan and Paul talked about the incident and she allayed his fears. He did indeed have a right to be safe and she was quite sure he would be safe with us. At the same time she made Paul aware that this did not mean he would be allowed to do as he liked. If he needed to be controlled, Neil and I would be prepared to do this. Finally, she emphasised that no one would be leaving the house, that Neil and I were both responsible for Paul and as his parents would continue to work together to provide him with a secure and stable home.

The incident was not only very significant for us, but it also shows what can happen when parents adopt a child like Paul. If I had been told before the placement that nine months later Neil would have threatened to hit Paul, I would have brushed aside the very idea. That Paul was able to push us to the limit of our tolerance was a salutary experience for both Neil and me. I have described the incident and subsequent discussion with Susan in some detail in the hope that this may help other foster and adoptive parents caught up in similar situations. I also hope they will find some reassurance in the sensitive way Susan treated what she clearly saw as an accident.

After such a traumatic 'down', the next few weeks certainly provided a welcome 'up'. Paul behaved better at school and at home.

We were all looking forward to his first Christmas with us. We were nervous that he might react badly to the disruption to his routine and to John and Margaret joining us, but on the whole he coped well and he really appreciated all his presents. Christmas was a wonderful time.

10

A New Year

New Year 1989 began with a feeling of hope. I was certain that if we could only resolve the school situation, Paul was well on the way to becoming a reasonably adjusted boy. There had been another change of headmistress at Christmas and the assistant head, Paul's own teacher who had been so understanding towards him, was taking over temporarily. Although we knew that Paul would have to get used to a new class teacher, and anticipated problems there, we were particularly heartened when the acting head told us she planned to deal with future suspensions by keeping him in a room in the school on his own rather than sending him home. That way, we all hoped bad behaviour would not be rewarded.

We were still buoyed up the day we went to Register House in Edinburgh with Paul to ask for a copy of his adoption certificate. We had decided we wanted something more concrete than Susan's letter to show Paul that we were now his parents. We were determined to make it a special day for him, and indeed it was. Paul looked quite awed as he entered Register House armed with his money and his letter of adoption, and we had to help him make his request. I was slightly disappointed that we were not given the certificate there and then, but Paul seemed quite content to wait for it to be posted to him and he was in a marvellous mood all day. He skipped and jumped round Edinburgh, seemed particularly close to us and was delighted when we gave him a card saying "Thanks for being our son". One of the delights of Paul is that he takes such pleasure in these situations and appreciates even small tokens of our love and commitment to him.

Alas, Paul was not at a stage where he could sustain good behaviour for any length of time. His deterioration now was partly due to the fact that we had decided to move house. Our present home was too small. Paul had moved into John's old bedroom and so John had to sleep in the study when he came home. This was obviously not satisfactory for John but, just as important, Paul's room had never really been his. He had, of course, furnished it with his own things, but it was still essentially John's room. A move to another house, more suitable for John's needs, would give Paul the opportunity to have his own room from the beginning. We also thought that moving house together would make him feel more a part of the family and less of an outsider. He could not say that everyone else had been there longer and had more right to be there. The new home would be a first for us all.

We were aware, however, that in the short term the move could be very disturbing to Paul. Every other move in his life had meant not only a change of house but a change of situation — of home, carer, environment, school — from parents, to foster parents, to the children's home, to our house. He had always had the feeling of moving into the unknown, that he had little control over events. The constant stream of potential purchasers, poking and peering into all the rooms, including his, probably also upset him. His tantrums increased and his sexual behaviour became much more explicit. I had accepted that when Paul felt insecure he would respond sexually. After all, his past experience had taught him to equate sexual behaviour with affection and I knew it would be a long time before Paul could show affection in different ways, particularly during periods of stress.

At school, too, Paul's behaviour inevitably worsened. I had told the headmistress about the likely effect of the move, but unfortunately when it came to the point one month into the new term and Paul was again faced with a suspension, she did not keep him in school. Paul had been disruptive in class and cheeky to the janitor during the morning break. He was sent to the headmistress who reprimanded him and told him to sit outside her room. Instead he went straight out into the playground. The headmistress rounded on him with exactly the sort of remarks designed to make Paul over-react: "You're letting your parents down", "You don't deserve a nice home and nice parents". Paul did not need to be told that he did not deserve nice things. He already believed that. He did not need to be told he was letting us down. He had such low self-esteem that he could not fail to feel that he was. He responded by being rude to the headmistress who suspended him for four weeks. She told us that, despite her previous commitment, she could not keep him within the school for this length of time. She could not guarantee that Paul would not disobey her again and that he would not walk out of school during suspension. Although we were prepared to take responsibility for his safety, she was adamant that he had to be suspended for four weeks.

Both Neil and I were totally despondent as we took Paul home from school. If he could not be maintained within mainstream education, the authorities could make decisions about his education which would threaten our role as his primary carers. After all we had been through with Paul, trying to settle him into our family, we were appalled that he might, for example, have to be sent to a residential school. Paul seemed totally unconcerned about the situation, unconcerned that yet again he had been suspended and unconcerned about the implications of this. Not only did he seem unable to cope in a school setting, but he lacked the motivation even to make an effort. The only hope we had of improving the situation was to get Paul to the stage where his commitment to us mattered enough for him not to want to risk it by misbehaviour at school. But we knew this stage was very far away and that Paul would continue to thwart our attempts to encourage good behaviour in school.

That night when we tried to talk to Paul and to get him to express some commitment to us, he replied that he did not care about anything or anyone, that he never had and never would, that he lived in a world of his own and nobody could get into it. He implied that this world had been a feature of his life for as long as he could remember. I was dumbfounded by this. I felt that Paul's aggression showed that he was very much part of this world, the world of other people, and that his aggression was his attempt to influence the world, to show it that he had the ability to fight back against what it had done to hurt him. I think to a large extent that my assessment was correct. Yet at the same time I accepted that Paul was able to retreat into his own world when things became too difficult. My worry was that this retreat would become the solution to all difficulties and that Paul wold turn into one of those withdrawn children who are not able to relate to those around him.

Paul was adamant that 'living in his world' was a self-protective measure which he used to avoid being hurt. When his parents had sent him to his room or locked him in cupboards, 'living in his own world' had made these occasions relatively pleasant for him. I told Paul that I could understand this and also why he might want to retreat into his own world when he was with us: he might be afraid to care about anything lest it be taken away from him and that would cause him hurt. When I asked Paul how often he went into a world of his own, he replied that he lived in it all the time. There was too much fight in Paul for me to believe this but I did not challenge his statement. I wanted to focus instead on the reasons for his private world. I asked Paul to think of something in his past which had made him sad. He told us about a budgie called Scruffy which he had when he was about three years old. Paul would play with the budgie and the budgie would squawk back. The noise upset his mother and one night when she was drunk she told Paul that if the budgie did not stop squawking she would kill it. The following morning when Paul got up it was dead. His mother had "murdered" it. Paul could see feathers and blood in the sink. When he challenged his mother she admitted killing the budgie but blamed Paul for the bird's death because he had made it squawk. Paul was crying while he recounted this story.

Paul went on to talk, for the first time, about his dad's illness and death. Apparently both his mother and grandmother had told Paul that his father's illness was partly the result of the strain imposed by Paul's behaviour which even then was very difficult. Although he did not say as much, I think he accepted that he was therefore to blame for his dad's death. What he did say was that he felt sad when his dad died, and when I asked him if he still missed his dad Paul said he did and became very upset. I would have loved to have put my arms round him and comforted him, but I felt it was more important that he should begin to come to terms with his grief at all his losses, that he should feel the hurt which is part of being in the real world and yet know he could cope with it.

There was no point in trying to minimise Paul's pain or tell him that he should not feel guilty. He would not have believed me or felt any better. So I decided to share some of the pain I had experienced. I reminded Paul that my dad was also dead and told him that it was I who had found him lying dead in the house. I had been late home and felt that if I had got back earlier I might have prevented his death. I told Paul that I had coped with this by creating a bubble round myself, just as he had. It was very comforting to be inside a bubble but eventually I knew I had to break it and face reality in the shape of my sadness and guilt. It was very painful at first, but I began to accept what other people had said, that I was not to blame for my father's death. Although I still felt sad about it, I was able to remember the nice things about him and this made me happier.

106

I told Paul that it was perhaps time he too left his world, however painful this might be, and I reminded him that the real world was often very good. If he came into it, he could be safe in the knowledge that despite his losses in the past, neither Neil nor I nor his possessions would be taken away from him. Paul stopped crying and said that he would try to live in the real world. We talked about other subjects and after a while Paul told me that he had been in the real world for fifteen minutes and it was all right. I said how pleased I was and left it at that.

Next morning we went to the school to discuss the situation. Any hopes we had of persuading the headmistress to reconsider her four-week suspension from the school were quickly dispelled. Nor was she prepared to reduce the period of suspension. Our only option was to transfer Paul to a new school.

It was with very mixed feelings that we made this decision. The present school had been sympathetic and tolerant towards Paul. He knew his teachers and fellow pupils and, up to a point, they had learned to manage his behaviour. Moving him might give him the idea that he could run away from difficulties. On the other hand, he showed no signs whatsoever of improvement and we knew that if we returned him to the school after the four weeks he would only be suspended again. Neil and I were doubtful whether a new school would work any better, but there was a primary with a male headteacher which seemed to offer most hope. We were keen the transfer should take place as soon as possible, so that Paul would not be rewarded with time off school. The headmistress was most helpful in expediting our plans and the very next day Paul started at his new school, in a class with a male teacher who had experience of teaching disturbed children.

What did Paul feel? Obviously he was apprehensive about another change in his life and peeved that he was not being allowed four weeks off school. What he really objected to, though, was being placed in Primary 6. We had arranged this to give us the option of delaying Paul's transfer to High School for a year without subjecting him to the indignity of other children knowing that he had been kept back. It provided the breathing space, if necessary, to help him work through his behaviourial problems in a primary environment before moving on to the challenges of High School. But Paul saw it as a major blow to his pride. It implied that he was too stupid to be in Primary 7. I had to spend several hours stressing that he was a bright, intelligent child and that the decision to place him in Primary 6 was in no way related to his ability at classwork. His problem was behaviour and, since he would cope easily with the work of Primary 6, he would have more time and energy to practise behaviour. Paul eventually accepted this, but over the next few weeks he needed constant reassurance that he was 'clever', as well as the promise that if he behaved well he could transfer to High School at the beginning of the next academic year.

We crossed our fingers that a fresh start at a new school would break the cycle of bad behaviour and motivate Paul to try harder. Our hopes were realised. Paul settled down well without any serious behaviourial problems. We began to relax slightly. It was so refreshing not having to telephone school every day. Paul too seemed happier, perhaps because he was no longer seen as the 'baddy' by other children and teachers and expected to misbehave. Miraculously, this good start was maintained and Paul completed the academic year without even one major outburst in school. It was the first significant breakthrough in Paul's ability to cope with the outside world.

The next two important landmarks were Paul's birthday and the first anniversary of his coming to live with us. We had decided to make his birthday a very special occasion for him. As well as a joint present, Neil and I each gave him an individual present. Paul was thrilled and spontaneously ran up and hugged us, with a "Thank you, mum and dad". That night we took him out for a meal. A birthday banner with a pig holding a message, "You're very special", was on the table when we arrived at the restaurant. Paul loved this, and as he tucked into smoked salmon, sirloin steak and gateau, I could not help reflecting that a year before Paul would not even have gone into a hotel or restaurant because it was "too snobby". Now he appreciated every moment, without any such misgivings. The arrival of the cake and the waitress singing "Happy Birthday to You" ended a superb day.

The next day, however, was not so good. After coping so well, his behaviour reverted — just as it had shortly after our successful Christmas. He had one tantrum after another and even kicked a hole in the door. Eventually Paul managed to explain what the trouble was. He had really enjoyed his birthday but simply because he had never had such a nice birthday before, surely it was obvious that he did not deserve one now? My heart went out to him. How sad to have reached eleven without ever having had a special birthday and, even sadder, still to feel so insecure that he genuinely believed he did not deserve it. I did my best to challenge his assumption that because of what had happened to him in the past, he deserved to be treated badly now, but, as always, I had some difficulty in convincing Paul that he deserved good things and his feeling of insecurity persisted for some time. He was quite bereft, for example, at the thought that I might go for a hillwalking weekend without him and acted as though I was about to desert him.

On Paul's first anniversary with us — 19 March — we bought him a cake in the shape of a number one and had a celebration at home. Again Paul lapped up the attention, and this time there were no bad repercussions, no tantrums, the following day. But the significance of being with us for one full year did not seem to register with Paul as it did with Neil and me. We had expected some noticeable changes in behaviour. We also anticipated a change, probably a deterioration, after about fifteen months (the time when his previous placement had broken down). In fact, there were no dramatic improvements or deteriorations in Paul's behaviour at either of these times. He seemed happier and more settled at home as well as school. He was looking forward to moving house and began to think what he would like for his new room. His sexual and regressive behaviour diminished and he was becoming somewhat closer to Neil. There were even a few occasions when he preferred Neil's company to mine. He cried more over events in the past and even his tantrums seemed less negative and more therapeutic. But these were only relative improvements. Paul was still a very demanding and difficult child.

At Easter I took Paul on holiday to Aviemore and was very disappointed that his behaviour was just as horrendous as on previous holidays. On one occasion he even put his feet through the windscreen of my car. Once again, I was heartily glad to return home from holiday. In contrast, Paul's holiday in Skye with Neil in May was much more successful. It was also the first long break I had had from Paul since he came to stay with us. The fourteen months had taken their toll on me, quite how much I only appreciated after a whole week without any pressures. When Neil and Paul arrived home and were telling me about the holiday, it became clear that Paul had had no tantrums during the entire time they were away.

I suggested that perhaps he was beginning to feel more settled with us and so no longer needed to have tantrums. Paul agreed: "I think you're right, mum."

I was not naïve enough to believe that Paul's problems were about to be magically cured. I knew he would continue to have difficulties at home, in school, in the outside world and that there would be times when I would despair whether he would ever improve; but I also knew what a struggle it had been for him to reach the point where he felt at home with us. When we moved house in June we did so as a family and Paul's words and behaviour told me that our new home was as much his as ours.

POSTSCRIPT

If I was asked to sum up the events since June 1989 the title of Chapter 9, Ups and Downs, would fit well. Paul has continued to make progress, but problems still persist. He went through a period of stealing, from me and from my mother. Although his tantrums became less frequent and his level of aggression was usually verbal, physical confrontations were more difficult to control. Paul grew bigger (he is now six feet tall) and stronger. On one occasion he threatened me with an axe; on other occasions he gave me a black eye, hacked a dent in my car and wrecked the central heating system. Holiday periods continue to be difficult, and there were times when I had to involve the police.

Paul's sexual behaviour virtually disappeared only to re-emerge during early adolescence. When he exposed himself to me and forced sexual advances on me, I was naturally extremely upset, but I quickly stopped this behaviour by confronting Paul about it in front of Neil. I was acting on the premise that if it is right for children to tell if they are being abused, it must also be right for adults. After this Paul wrote my mother a letter saying he wanted to have sex with her because he loved her. In school he touched a girl's breasts. He was obviously having difficulty in recognising the parameters of appropriate behaviour.

School also had its ups and downs. Paul's teacher and headmaster felt he was ready to move to High School in August 1989. He settled well at first, but then problems began and approximately nine months into his first year we again had to change schools. He did not last long in the new school and in February 1991, after several suspensions, we had to remove Paul from mainstream education. He is now attending a residential school during the week.

In November 1991 the strain on Neil's and my relationship came to a head and we decided to separate.

However, all is not doom and gloom. Paul is coping reasonably well in his new school and I have hopes that he may soon be able to

111

return to mainstream education. He is receiving psychological treatment to help him come to terms with his past, and there has been no repetition of his sexual behaviour. Even my separation from Neil has had its positive side in that Paul has become much more settled at home, partly, I imagine, because there is less tension in the house and partly because he now has little competition for my attention.

Sometimes when Paul is behaving badly it is difficult to remember all the improvements he has made. Sometimes, I must admit, I have despaired but in the main I feel optimistic about the future. I certainly do not in any way regret my decision to adopt a child.

Let me end with a dream. Some months after coming to live with us Paul and I were discussing our dreams. He told me that the night after he first met me he dreamt about someone coming into his room. The person floated in through his bedroom window and was very frightening. It carried a knife and Paul knew that it wanted to kill him. As it moved closer and became more threatening, Paul realised that the person was me. He had the same dream the day he came to live with us, but never since. Could you, I ask, have the strength to conquer this level of fear and still come and live with us? Thank you, Paul.

The Children's Society

The Children's Society is a national voluntary organisation of the Church of England and the Church in Wales. It exists to work with children and young people, irrespective of their race or religious belief:
- to help them grow in their families and communities
- to help them take charge of their own lives
- to help them to change the conditions that stand in their way.

The Children's Society runs more than 150 projects throughout England and Wales including:
- family centres and neighbourhood groups in local communities where families are under stress often feeling isolated and powerless to improve their lives
- helping children and young people with special needs to find new families
- working with young people living on the street
- providing independent living units for young people leaving care
- working with young offenders, offering them a constructive alternative to crime
- residential and day care for young people with disabilities
- promoting children's and young people's rights.

The Children's Society is also committed to raising public awareness of issues affecting children and young people and to promoting the welfare and rights of children and young people in matters of public policy.

For further information about the work of The Children's Society, please contact:
The Information Department
The Children's Society
Edward Rudolf House
Margery Street
London WC1X 0JL
Tel. 071-837 4299

Other titles available from The Children's Society

The Children's Society publishes a wide range of books, booklets and resource packs. Listed below is a selection of titles:

Bruce's Story
A colourful story book for children experiencing disruption in their lives — moving to a new foster or adoptive family, or starting in a new school.
(Price £4.25)

Into Pandora's Box
A collection of poems written by a survivor of child sexual abuse.
(Price £6.50)

Working With Sexually Abused Children: a resource pack for professionals
Includes story books, leaflets, and a colouring book, all aimed at children and young people; and a series of nine practice papers.
(Complete pack £26.75; items may be ordered individually)

Tough Love
A personal account of being in care and of moving to live independently, written by a young man who went into care at the age of three. (Price £5.50)

Dennis Duckling
An illustrated story book for young children who are entering care or joining a new foster or adoptive family. (Price £2.00)

Preparation for Independent Living
A report by The Children's Society's Battersea Bedsit Project. It has been written jointly by staff and young people resident at the project who have been in care and are preparing to move on. It also offers a model of work for other practitioners working with young people.
(Price £6.00)

Education for Citizenship

A resource pack for 11-14-year-olds containing more than 50 varied activities on five broad themes: families and care; young people and the law; young people's rights; poverty; and homes and homelessness. Suitable for use in schools or youth groups. (Price £19.95)

Divorce and Children

A pack of three leaflets and a briefing paper for parents and children experiencing divorce, and for those working with them. (Price £1.00)

Family Homelessness Pack

Contains a video made by children living in bed and breakfast accommodation; a study in family homelessness in Thanet, Kent; and a briefing paper giving a national perspective on the issues and details of the work of Children's Society projects. (Complete pack £15.00; items may be ordered individually)

Further information on these titles and a full publications list are available from:

The Publications Department
The Children's Society
Edward Rudolf House
Margery Street
London WC1X 0JL
Tel. 071-837 4299; fax 071-837 0211.